ENGAGING IN COGNITIVELY COMPLEX TASKS

CLASSROOM TECHNIQUES TO HELP STUDENTS GENERATE & TEST HYPOTHESES ACROSS DISCIPLINES

D1445254

ENGAGING IN COGNITIVELY COMPLEX TASKS

CLASSROOM TECHNIQUES TO HELP STUDENTS GENERATE & TEST HYPOTHESES ACROSS DISCIPLINES

Deana Senn
Robert J. Marzano

With Carla Moore and Penny L. Sell

1400 Centrepark Blvd, Suite 1000
West Palm Beach, FL 33401
717-845-6300

email: pub@learningsciences.com
learningsciences.com

Printed in the United States of America

20 19 18 17 16 15   3 4 5

FSC
www.fsc.org
MIX
Paper from
responsible sources
FSC® C005010

Publisher's Cataloging-in-Publication Data

Senn, Deana.
   Engaging in cognitively complex tasks: classroom techniques to help students generate & test hypotheses / Deana Senn [and] Robert J. Marzano.
      pages cm. – (Essentials for achieving rigor series)
   ISBN: 978-1-941112-09-0 (pbk.)
1. Critical thinking—Study and teaching. 2. Cognitive learning. 3. Effective teaching—United States. 5. Learning, Psychology of. I. Marzano, Robert J. II. Title.
   LB1025.3 . S447 2014
   370.15—dc23
                              [2014939915]

MARZANO CENTER

Essentials for Achieving Rigor SERIES

The *Essentials for Achieving Rigor* series of instructional guides helps educators become highly skilled at implementing, monitoring, and adapting instruction. Put it to practical use immediately, adopting day-to-day examples as models for application in your own classroom.

Books in the series:

Identifying Critical Content: Classroom Techniques to Help Students Know What Is Important

Examining Reasoning: Classroom Techniques to Help Students Produce and Defend Claims

Recording & Representing Knowledge: Classroom Techniques to Help Students Accurately Organize and Summarize Content

Examining Similarities & Differences: Classroom Techniques to Help Students Deepen Their Understanding

Processing New Information: Classroom Techniques to Help Students Engage With Content

Revising Knowledge: Classroom Techniques to Help Students Examine Their Deeper Understanding

Practicing Skills, Strategies & Processes: Classroom Techniques to Help Students Develop Proficiency

Engaging in Cognitively Complex Tasks: Classroom Techniques to Help Students Generate & Test Hypotheses Across Disciplines

Creating & Using Learning Targets & Performance Scales: How Teachers Make Better Instructional Decisions

Organizing for Learning: Classroom Techniques to Help Students Interact Within Small Groups

Dedication

I dedicate this work to my parents, Lucie Verbois and George Senn, who raised me to take care and take risk (not necessarily in that order), and to my other parents, Kay Senn and Marvin Verbois, who also love and support me.

—Deana Senn

Table of Contents

Acknowledgments

Learning Sciences International would like to thank the following reviewers:

Christopher Bowen
2014 Tennessee Teacher of the Year
  Finalist
Liberty Bell Middle School
Johnson City, Tennessee

Todd E. Chappa
2014 Michigan Teacher of the Year
  Finalist
Lake Center Elementary
Portage, Michigan

Melissa Collins
2014 West Tennessee Teacher
  of the Year
John P. Freeman Optional School
Memphis, Tennessee

Elizabeth Day
2005 New York Teacher of the Year
Mechanicville Central
  School District
Mechanicville, New York

Allison Fredericks
Math Teacher
Dr. David L. Anderson Middle School
Stuart, Florida

Laura Holling
English Language Arts Team Leader
Martin County High School
Stuart, Florida

Katherine Koch-Laveen
2001 Minnesota Teacher of the Year
Apple Valley High School
Apple Valley, Minnesota

Derek Minakami
  2001 Hawaii Teacher of the Year/
  Principal
Kaneohe Elementary School
Kaneohe, Hawaii

Jon Parrott
2014 Iowa Teacher of the Year
  Finalist
Urbandale High School
Urbandale, Iowa

Chris Pruss
Director of Literacy K–8
Danbury Public Schools
Danbury, Connecticut

Tiffany Richard
2012 Kansas Teacher of the Year
Olathe East High School
Olathe, Kansas

Meg Strnat
2014 Indiana Teacher of the Year
  Finalist
Cumberland Road Elementary
  School
Fishers, Indiana

About the Authors

DEANA SENN, MSSE, is an expert in instructional strategies and classroom assessments. She is the Instructional Designer and Staff Developer for Learning Sciences International. Ms. Senn's curriculum, instruction, and assessment experience spans the United States and Canada. Ms. Senn has been a teacher and leader in school, district, regional, and provincial roles in both rural and urban settings. She is a graduate of Texas A&M University and received her master's degree from Montana State University. With her extensive experience focusing on teaching and learning, Ms. Senn offers a unique perspective for improving instructional practice.

ROBERT J. MARZANO, PhD, is CEO of Marzano Research Laboratory and Executive Director of the Learning Sciences Marzano Center for Teacher and Leader Evaluation. A leading researcher in education, he is a speaker, trainer, and author of more than 150 articles on topics such as instruction, assessment, writing and implementing standards, cognition, effective leadership, and school intervention. He has authored over 30 books, including *The Art and Science of Teaching* (ASCD, 2007) and *Teacher Evaluation That Makes a Difference* (ASCD, 2013).

CARLA MOORE, MSEd, is an experienced professional developer, teacher, and administrator who oversees content and product development for Learning Sciences International, with a special emphasis on teacher and administrator effectiveness. Formerly, she was the Director of Quality Instruction at St. Lucie County Public Schools in Florida, coleading the implementation of the Marzano Teacher Evaluation Model and supporting training within the district. She is the recipient of the 2013 Florida Association of Staff Development Award, the Schlechty Centre Conference Fellowship, and the Treasure Coast News Lifetime Achiever of Education Award, among others.

PENNY SELL, MSEd, has spent more than 30 years in public education, and her roles have included teacher, administrator, trainer, and consultant. She earned her bachelor's degree in exceptional education from Central Michigan University and her master's degree in educational leadership from the University of Central Florida.

Introduction

This guide, *Engaging in Cognitively Complex Tasks: Classroom Techniques to Help Students Generate & Test Hypotheses Across Disciplines*, is intended as a resource for improving a specific aspect of instructional practice: helping students utilize their knowledge.

Your motivation to incorporate this strategy into your instructional toolbox may have come from a personal desire to improve your instructional practice through the implementation of a research-based set of strategies (such as those found in the Marzano instructional framework) or a desire to increase the rigor of the instructional strategies you implement in your classroom so that students meet the expectations of demanding standards such as the Common Core State Standards, Next Generation Science Standards, C3 Framework for Social Studies State Standards, or state standards based on or influenced by College and Career Readiness Anchor Standards.

This guide will help teachers of all grade levels and subjects improve their performance of a specific instructional strategy: engaging in cognitively complex tasks. Narrowing your focus on a specific skill, such as cognitively complex tasks, permits you to concentrate on the nuances of this instructional strategy to deliberately improve it. This allows you to intentionally plan, implement, monitor, adapt, and reflect on this single element of your instructional practice. A person seeking to become an expert displays very distinctive behaviors, as explained by Marzano and Toth (2013):

- breaks down the specific skills required to be an expert

- focuses on improving those particular critical skill chunks (as opposed to easy tasks) during practice or day-to-day activities

- receives immediate, specific, and actionable feedback, particularly from a more experienced coach

- continually practices each critical skill at more challenging levels with the intention of mastering it, giving far less time to skills already mastered

This series of guides will support each of the previously listed behaviors, with a focus on breaking down the specific skills required to be an expert and giving day-to-day practical suggestions to enhance these skills.

Building on the Marzano Instructional Model

This series is based on the Marzano instructional framework, which is grounded in research and provides educators with the tools they need to connect instructional practice to student achievement. The series uses key terms that are specific to the Marzano model of instruction. See Table 1, Glossary of Key Terms.

Table 1: Glossary of Key Terms

Term	Definition
CCSS	Common Core State Standards is the official name of the standards documents developed by the Common Core State Standards Initiative (CCSSI), the goal of which is to prepare students in the United States for college and career.
CCR	College and Career Readiness Anchor Standards are broad statements that incorporate individual standards for various grade levels and specific content areas.
Desired result	The intended result for the student(s) due to the implementation of a specific strategy.
Monitoring	The act of checking for evidence of the desired result of a specific strategy while the strategy is being implemented.
Instructional strategy	A category of techniques used for classroom instruction that has been proven to have a high probability of enhancing student achievement.
Instructional technique	The method used to teach and deepen understanding of knowledge and skills.
Content	The knowledge and skills necessary for students to demonstrate standards.
Scaffolding	A purposeful progression of support that targets cognitive complexity and student autonomy to reach rigor.
Extending	Activities that move students who have already demonstrated the desired result to a higher level of understanding.

The educational pendulum swings widely from decade to decade. Educators move back and forth between prescriptive checklists and step-by-step lesson plans to approaches that encourage instructional autonomy with minimal regard for the science of teaching and need for accountability. Two practices are often missing in both of these approaches to defining effective instruction: 1) specific statements of desired results, and 2) solid research-based connections. The Marzano instructional framework provides a comprehensive system that details what is required from teachers to develop their craft using research-based instructional strategies. Launching from this solid instructional foundation, teachers will then be prepared to merge that science with their own unique, yet effective, instructional style, which is the art of teaching.

Engaging in Cognitively Complex Tasks: Classroom Techniques to Help Students Generate & Test Hypotheses Across Disciplines will help you grow into an innovative and highly skilled teacher who is able to implement, scaffold, and extend instruction to meet a range of student needs.

Essentials for Achieving Rigor

This series of guides details essential classroom strategies to support the complex shifts in teaching that are necessary for an environment where academic rigor is a requirement for all students. The instructional strategies presented in this series are essential to effectively teach the CCSS, the Next Generation Science Standards, or standards designated by your school district or state. They require a deeper understanding, more effective use of strategies, and greater frequency of implementation for your students to demonstrate the knowledge and skills required by rigorous standards. This series includes instructional techniques appropriate for all grade levels and content areas. The examples contained within are grade-level specific and should serve as models and launching points for application in your own classroom.

Your skillful implementation of these strategies is essential to your students' mastery of the CCSS or other rigorous standards, no matter the grade level or subject you are teaching. Other instructional strategies covered in the Essentials for Achieving Rigor series, such as examining reasoning and identifying critical content, exemplify the cognitive complexity needed to meet rigorous standards. Taken as a package, these strategies may at first glance seem quite daunting. For this reason, the series focuses on just one strategy in each guide.

In the context of teaching students information, engaging in cognitively complex tasks is essential to learning in a rigorous classroom. As you become more skilled in implementing this strategy, you will see remarkable changes in your students' abilities to use the information they have learned in your classroom. You will have a classroom of students who not only understand essential knowledge required by the standards but also can use that knowledge in novel situations. Whether a given standard is part of the CCSS or a set of district or state standards, your students will benefit from your expertise at engaging them in cognitively complex tasks. Picture the ultimate goal you have in mind for your students: the successful application of the knowledge and skills they have. This instructional strategy focuses on showing students how to use their acquired knowledge in more cognitively complex ways.

Engaging in Cognitively Complex Tasks

The cognitively complex tasks referred to in the title of this book demand higher-level thinking skills from your students, skills that ultimately lead to the generation and testing of hypotheses about knowledge they have acquired in your classroom. These types of challenging tasks require that students make decisions, solve problems, experiment, or investigate, and teachers do not readily observe these skills in classrooms (Marzano & Toth, 2014).

For students, the core of effectively engaging in cognitively complex tasks is the ability to produce and support claims. You and your students must master a structured and rigorous method for producing and supporting claims that includes these steps: 1) state a claim, 2) establish grounds, 3) provide backing, and 4) frame qualifiers to include describing counterarguments as well as identifying one or more of the four types of thinking errors (faulty logic, errors of attack, weak reference, or misinformation). Once students are familiar with the vocabulary and thinking processes necessary for producing and supporting claims in sources and content the teacher provides, they will be ready to tackle the more demanding task of generating and testing their own hypotheses about prior knowledge using techniques such as decision making and problem solving.

If you have not previously taught your students how to formally state and support claims, an earlier book in this series, *Examining Reasoning*, describes several techniques in which students learn how to support claims and assertions with evidence, produce and defend claims related to content, identify and analyze claims in an author's work, and judge reasoning and evidence in an author's work. These techniques lay the foundation by showing students how to engage in the thinking process of producing and supporting claims as a critical aspect of understanding and deepening their content knowledge. They prepare students for the rigor required for a new level of thinking: producing their own claims about content as well as generating and testing original hypotheses related to their content knowledge.

To fully understand this strategy, consider its context in a typical learning cycle or instructional sequence. Within every learning cycle, the effective teacher uses various instructional strategies that intentionally move students toward more cognitively complex tasks and increasing levels of responsibility for their own thinking and learning. Your ultimate goal is that students will be able to engage in cognitively complex tasks related to critical content.

Note that students need to learn, practice, and deepen their understanding of content before you can expect them to utilize that knowledge to generate and test hypotheses. When implementing various instructional strategies, teachers should identify and plan for the interdependence and cumulative effect among instructional strategies. An example of interdependence can be explained in this short summary: Once a teacher identifies the *critical content*, the next step is to *chunk* that critical content and *preview* it with students. The teacher will then ask students to *process* that content. After students process the content, she further extends understanding by asking questions that require students to make inferences, or *elaborate*, about content. If the teacher desires to monitor whether students have internalized the critical content, she may ask them to *record*, *represent*, and even *reflect* on this knowledge. Then she might ask students to *examine their reasoning* about the content.

The italicized instructional strategies are not executed, nor do they have their intended effects, in isolation. Rather, a teacher with an instructional repertoire skillfully blends the strategies to achieve the overarching desired results.

Throughout learning, but most especially at the culmination of a specific learning sequence such as a unit or chapter, students should engage in activities that require them to experiment with their own knowledge and skills. In the course of producing and supporting claims *and* generating and testing hypotheses, students move beyond basic levels of knowing and gain the abilities and confidence to analyze their own understanding of content in novel situations.

The Effective Implementation of Engaging in Cognitively Complex Tasks

There are two aspects to the effective implementation of engaging students in cognitively complex tasks: 1) fully understand the process for producing and supporting claims, which lies at the core of this instructional strategy, and 2) thoughtfully consider the logistics of implementation.

Understand the Process for Producing and Supporting Claims

The effective implementation of engaging in cognitively complex tasks requires a basic understanding of the process for producing and supporting claims. If you are not familiar with the techniques presented in *Examining Reasoning,* Table 2 describes the steps and vocabulary associated with stating and supporting claims that you will find used and described in more detail in the techniques in this book.

Table 2: How Students Produce and Support Claims

Step	Definition	Example	Teacher's Notes
State a claim	Students state claims based on their previous understanding (prior learning) of the content. They derive their claims in two ways: 1) based on the knowledge about content they have acquired and deepened to this point and 2) in response to a prompt or leading question about the content the teacher provides.	The Battle of Britain was the pivotal battle of World War II.	Students must produce their claims before they begin looking for evidence in support of their claims.
Establish grounds	Students collect evidence in support of their claims. This evidence is labeled *grounds.* Grounds contain the strongest and most persuasive evidence.	If Britain had been knocked out of the war, Germany could then have focused all of its resources on defeating the Soviet Union.	Evidence in support of students' claims can be one of four types: 1) common knowledge, 2) expert opinion, 3) experimental evidence, and 4) factual information.

(continued on next page)

Table 2: How Students Produce and Support Claims (continued)

Step	Definition	Example	Teacher's Notes
Provide backing	Students collect additional information about grounds that establish their validity. The backing is based on evidence unearthed through observation or investigation.	The British Isles could not have been used for staging during Operation Overlord.	The provision of backing will depend on the content, the complexity of the claim, and your students' ability to sustain more extensive research into additional resources.
Frame the qualifiers	Students collect evidence that serves as qualifiers. Qualifying evidence is used to determine the strength of the students' claims and consider the degree to which the countervailing evidence undermines or weakens their claims. The process of framing qualifiers can also include identifying common thinking errors that may weaken counterarguments.	There were other major countries battling Germany, and there were other fronts on which the war was being waged.	Qualifiers are an important aspect of stating and supporting claims. They serve to help students understand that the process of stating and supporting claims is more than finding supportive evidence. It also includes accounting for contradictory or confusing evidence that cannot be ignored. The common logical errors that are qualifiers to students' claims include limits of statistical information, faulty logic, attack, weak reference, and misinformation.

Adapted from Marzano (2007), Marzano & Heflebower (2012), and Ocasio & Marzano (2015).

Thoughtfully Consider the Logistics of Implementation

There are several logistics to consider if you are to effectively implement the techniques in this book: 1) the degree of choice you will grant to your students, 2) the degree of autonomy you will cede to your students, 3) the amount of time you will allocate for the collection of evidence, 4) the types of guidance you will provide to students, 5) the kind and amount of resources you will provide, and 6) the overall duration of the cognitively complex task. While you may not fully understand or appreciate all of these considerations before you implement, use them to mentally walk yourself through the various lesson examples with your students and content in mind.

The Degree of Choice You Will Grant to Your Students

Grant students some choices during implementation, but provide boundaries to keep students focused. Provide a set of materials, resources, or specific guidelines to give parameters to their generation and testing of hypotheses. However, stop short of telling students the exact steps they need to take to prove or disprove their hypotheses.

The Degree of Autonomy You Will Cede to Your Students

When you implement a cognitively complex task for the first time, students will be uncertain about the process, especially if they are unaccustomed to making decisions about their own learning. In the beginning, devote more time to coaching and supporting them. Gradually, students will become more certain about your expectations, and you can then step back and let them work independently. Allow students time to ponder, debate, and even struggle a bit; however, do not ignore students' frustration indefinitely. The secret to effective implementation of a cognitively complex task is doing all you can to ensure your students are doing the thinking work.

The Amount of Time You Will Allocate for the Collection of Evidence

An important consideration in the implementation of this strategy is giving students adequate time to collect needed evidence to support a conclusion. Whether you are facilitating a short-term cognitively complex task or a longer-term project, students need time to reach their own conclusions and support them with evidence.

The Guidance and Facilitation You Will Provide to Students

Plan in advance how you will support students throughout each cognitively complex task. The first step in providing guidance and support is to ensure that all students understand the complex steps involved in the task. Prepare to provide both verbal and written directions at the beginning of a task. Some teachers like to have students paraphrase the directions before they start the task so they can ensure that all students know the steps.

As students engage in cognitively complex tasks, be a highly visible and interactive presence. Move about the classroom to assist and monitor. Ask guiding questions to support student engagement and higher-level thinking. Give ongoing feedback to students as they engage in the task. Ask probing questions, intentionally thinking about how you can facilitate rather than tell, and guide rather than lead.

The Kind and Amount of Resources You Will Provide to Students

Volunteer a variety of resources. Assist students as they analyze their thinking and draw conclusions. Their success depends on your facilitating their learning through coaching and support. Identify the resources your students will need, and if necessary, secure those resources for students in advance of the activity. For example, fill a library cart with potential sources and make them available during the task. If students need internet access, point them to the most applicable and appropriate websites. If you wish, provide some lesser-quality materials so that students can compare and select the best. The ultimate goal is that students will decide for themselves which information is valuable and use it to support or test their hypotheses.

The Overall Length of the Cognitively Complex Task

Cognitively complex tasks are often viewed as long-term projects that require hours of research or experimentation and multiple class days to complete. Some cognitively complex tasks do fall into that category. However, the generation and testing of hypotheses can also take place during short-term lessons that lay a foundation for success with cognitively complex tasks that are sustained over longer periods of time. There are examples of cognitively complex tasks that vary in length within each chapter of this book.

Teacher Actions Associated With the Effective Implementation of Cognitively Complex Tasks

There are many teacher actions associated with the effective implementation of cognitively complex tasks. This list is not exhaustive, but it represents the diversity and intricacy of behaviors you might use to teach, model, and support effective cognitively complex tasks:

- Think aloud for students as you read the prompt.

- Teach and model for students how to generate a hypothesis.

- Provide opportunities for students to read and discuss the merits of other hypotheses.

- Identify essential steps in testing hypotheses.

- Provide guidance as students plan how to test their hypotheses.

- Teach students how to document evidence that confirms or disconfirms their claims.

- Provide opportunities for students to examine and analyze the strength of support presented for a claim.

- Model how to create conclusions that explain whether students' hypotheses are confirmed or disconfirmed.

- Require students to support their conclusion with evidence.

- Circulate around the room to be readily available to students.

- Ask questions to help students think for themselves.

Common Mistakes

As you begin to implement this strategy, consider first how to avoid the following common mistakes. These errors can take your teaching, and ultimately students' learning, off course:

- The teacher fails to provide a prompt that requires a cognitively complex response.

- The teacher fails to expect all students to state a claim.

- The teacher fails to release responsibility to students to think independently.

- The teacher fails to follow the process through to its conclusion and evaluation after asking students to generate a hypothesis.

Failing to Provide a Prompt That Requires a Cognitively Complex Response

Since cognitively complex tasks are usually the most rigorous activity you will ask a student to perform within a typical learning cycle, ensure that the task is at the level of cognitive complexity you intend it to be, usually the same level of cognitive complexity as the learning target.

Failing to Expect All Students to State a Claim

When time is of the essence, you may be tempted to rely on the answers of a few students to represent the thinking of the class. What is essential, however, about producing claims or generating hypotheses is not that the class as a whole states a claim or generates a hypothesis, but that individual students have an opportunity to examine their own thinking to generate a hypothesis. Ensure that structures are in place so that all of your students have opportunities and guidance to state their own claim as they begin a cognitively complex task.

Failing to Expect and Then Allow Students to Think for Themselves

If students are unaccustomed to examining their own thinking, they may not know how to even begin the process. So, with the best of intentions, you may decide to move the process along by telling students what to think rather than guiding them to examine their own thinking. The goal of hypothesis generation and testing is that students will learn how to examine what they personally know or think about a topic. If you tell your students what to think and how to conduct a cognitively complex task, you will be doing their thinking for them.

Failing to Follow Through After Asking Students to Generate a Hypothesis

You undoubtedly use predicting (generating a hypothesis) as part of your usual questioning techniques. During a read-aloud, you might ask students to predict what is going to happen next to the main character. While conducting an experiment, you might ask students to predict what will happen when you mix two chemicals together. Those predictions, while important, are only a beginning step. In the context of engaging in cognitively complex tasks, you must expect students to follow through and examine whether the evidence supports or does not support their predictions.

Monitoring for the Desired Result

As your students work at various cognitively complex tasks, your top instructional priority is to monitor their progress. The extra attention you provide while students are working individually or in small groups will pay rich dividends in student learning. As students are engaged in implementing one of the techniques, check to see if an individual or all of the individuals in a small group can explain their hypotheses. Determine if the evidence they have documented truly supports the prediction or claim they stated at the outset of the task. Stay in constant touch with students who are prone to struggling and help them get unstuck so that they can make the most of their allocated work time. Be available to guide or redirect students if they appear to be heading off course. Students learn more and retain knowledge more readily when teachers give them opportunities to revise their work based on what they learn along the way. Following are some examples that can help you determine if your students are able to engage in cognitively complex tasks:

1. When prompted, students can explain the hypotheses they are testing.

2. Students are able to test their hypotheses.

3. Students can identify evidence that supports or refutes their hypotheses.

4. Students can explain whether their evidence confirmed or disconfirmed their hypotheses.

5. Students can explain how their evidence confirmed or disconfirmed their hypotheses.

6. Students can explain common logical errors that may affect their hypotheses.

Each technique described in this book has examples of monitoring specific to that technique.

Scaffolding and Extending Instruction to Meet Students' Needs

The purpose of monitoring is to collect evidence of your students' progress in implementing a specific technique. As you monitor, you will notice that some students are not able to complete a cognitively complex task without extensive support and guidance, while other students are quickly able to complete the cognitively complex task and need more challenges to use their knowledge in novel ways. Examples of how to scaffold and extend instruction are included as part of the explanation for each of the techniques.

Scaffolding provides support that targets cognitive complexity and student autonomy to reach rigor. There are four categories of support you can provide for students who need scaffolding (Dickson, Collins, Simmons & Kame'enui, 1998):

- enlisting help for students from their peers, instructional aides, or other paraprofessionals

- manipulating the difficulty level of content that you are teaching (for example, providing an easier reading level that contains the same content)

- breaking down the content into smaller chunks to make it more manageable

- giving students organizers to clarify and guide their thinking through a task one step at a time

Extending moves students who have already demonstrated the desired result to a higher level of understanding. These examples are provided as suggestions, and you adapt them to target the specific needs of your students. Use the scaffolding examples to spark ideas as you plan to meet the needs of your English language learners, students who receive special education or lack support, or simply the student who was absent the day before. The extension activities can help you plan for students in your gifted and talented program or those with a keen interest in the subject matter you are teaching who have already learned the fundamentals.

Teacher Self-Reflection

As with any skill you want to acquire or improve upon, reflecting is essential. The following set of questions begins with simply reflecting about how to begin the implementation process and moves to progressively more complex ways of helping students become autonomous learners as they generate and test hypotheses:

1. How can you ensure you and your students are incorporating the steps in each type of cognitively complex task your students are completing?

2. How can you provide resources and guidance to assist students with engaging in cognitively complex tasks?

3. How might you monitor the extent to which your students are able to analyze their own thinking as they generate and test hypotheses?

4. How might you adapt and create new strategies for cognitively complex tasks that address unique student needs and situations?

5. What are you learning about your students as you adapt and create new strategies?

Instructional Techniques to Engage Students in Cognitively Complex Tasks

There are many ways to engage students in cognitively complex tasks. The ways you choose to facilitate your students' examination of their ideas, thinking processes, and logic will depend on your grade level, content, and the makeup of your class. These various ways or options are called instructional techniques. In the subsequent chapters, you will find six techniques to engage students in cognitively complex tasks. They are listed here:

- Instructional Technique 1: Investigating

- Instructional Technique 2: Problem Solving

- Instructional Technique 3: Decision Making

- Instructional Technique 4: Experimental Inquiry

- Instructional Technique 5: Inventing

- Instructional Technique 6: Student-Designed Tasks

All of the techniques are similarly organized and include the following components:

- a brief introduction to the technique

- ways to effectively implement the technique

- common mistakes to avoid as you implement the technique

- examples and nonexamples from elementary and secondary classrooms using selected learning targets or standards from various documents

- ways to monitor for the desired result

- ways to scaffold and extend instruction to meet the needs of students

Instructional Technique 1

INVESTIGATING

In this technique, students generate and test a hypothesis by investigating what others have said or written about a specific idea, event, or concept. There are three types of investigations. Table 1.1 describes these types as well as lists some possible prompts you might use to motivate your students' thinking at the outset of the investigation process.

Table 1.1: Types of Investigations

Type of Investigation	Description of the Investigation	Suggested Prompts to Motivate the Investigation
Historical	Requires students to construct plausible scenarios for events from the past for which there is no general agreement among sources	• How did this happen? • Why did this happen? • Take a position on this event.
Projective	Requires students to use the knowledge they gain during an investigation to make projections on future or hypothetical events	• What would happen if . . . ? • Predict the resolution of . . . • Predict what might have happened if circumstances changed.
Definitional	Requires students to describe characteristics of places, things, or concepts	• What are the important features of . . . ? • What are the defining characteristics of . . . ? • What are the differing features of . . . ?

Adapted from Marzano (2007).

How to Effectively Implement Investigating

There are four steps to effectively implement investigations with your students: 1) use the provided planning template to walk through the various steps of the investigation; 2) teach and model the steps for how to generate and support claims, as shown earlier; 3) begin your investigation lesson with the prompt you have chosen; and 4) provide resources and guidance during the investigational task.

Use the Planning Template

Before introducing your students to one of the investigation techniques, review the planning template shown in Table 1.2. At first glance, the template may seem to be a lesson plan, but it is not. It is more like a "thinking" plan. The plan is divided into three parts. Part 1 of the plan contains the action steps that you will take *prior* to presenting a prompt or question to students. Your answers to these questions will help you identify critical aspects of the investigation. Your students will do the "thinking" work during this lesson. However, the technique will be successful only if you do *your* "thinking" homework in advance. Part 2 of the plan contains the action steps that students will follow as they generate and support claims based on the parameters of the investigation that you identify in Part 1. The planning questions in Part 2 are intended to alert you to the many decisions you must make in advance of implementation. Some of these considerations are in the introduction to the strategy. Part 3 includes two action steps that you will take during your students' investigation.

Table 1.2: A Planning Template for Investigating

1. Planning Questions for Teacher's Action Steps	
Identify the learning target	With what learning target is this task aligned?
Determine the topic	What topic do you want students to research? Does it align with the topic of the learning target?
Decide on the type of investigation	What type of investigation aligns best with the topic and the learning target? See Table 1.1 for descriptions of the various types of investigations.
Identify questions or prompts	What questions will you ask to prompt the investigation? Table 1.1 contains suggested prompts that align with the various types of investigations. Do your questions or prompts align with the level of cognition of the learning target?
2. Planning Questions for Students' Action Steps	
State a claim	How will you ask students to state the claim or respond to the question? (In groups? In their academic notebooks?)
Identify what is already known	What activities might you facilitate? What resources will you provide? How will your students document grounds and backing for their claims?
Identify confusion or contradictions	What directions will you include to help students identify confusions and contradictions?
Develop a plausible resolution	How will you prompt students to reach a conclusion? How will you ask students to support their conclusions with grounds, backing and qualifiers?
Reflect on the initial claim	How will you ask students to contrast their conclusions to their initial claims?
3. Planning Questions for Teacher's Action Steps During the Implementation	
Plan to monitor	How will you check that your students are analyzing their own thinking as they investigate?
Plan to adapt	What will you plan for students who need support or extension?

Teach and Model the Steps for Generating and Supporting Claims

Once you have taught and modeled the steps for this technique, they will easily adapt to the three types of investigations as well as the other techniques in the book.

1. **State a claim.**

    Students state precisely what they hope to prove in their investigation. The students should base their claims on what they have previously learned about a subject or an event.

2. **Identify what is already known.**

    Students begin the task by researching what is known about the subject. During this research, they gradually find information that will build support for their claims with evidence known as grounds and backing. Students can research by using articles or text you provide, or they can find the information on their own using both print and digital resources. If you use the latter approach, be sure you have taught students how to appropriately use digital resources. Do not provide students with the information they need. The point of the investigation is that students will seek out the information independently. The goal of the search for grounds, backing, and qualifiers is not that students will acquire more facts about a concept or event, although that may well happen in an incidental way as the process unfolds. The goal is to facilitate students in their abilities to engage in cognitively complex tasks. Throughout the research process, students need to synthesize the information they have found in their search, not simply restate it.

3. **Identify confusion or contradictions.**

    Students must identify any confusion or contradictions in the information that is already known and then determine which information best supports their claims. As students investigate, they may find sources that contradict each other or illuminate confusion that exists about a concept or event. Help your students understand that experts in a field can often contradict one another. This does not necessarily mean that a source is unreliable but rather that there are different accounts of the same situation or differing theories about the same concept. Your students should be prepared not only to identify these qualifiers but also point out common logical errors in the information.

4. **Develop a plausible resolution.**
    To support their original claims, students must develop a plausible resolution—a conclusion that responds to the original prompt, is supported by their interpretation of the evidence they have collected, and resolves any confusing or conflicting information.

5. **Reflect on the initial claim.**
    Students contrast their conclusions with the initial claims they stated. Help students understand that the information they have gathered may not always support their claims. Students do not need to revise their claims, nor should you base their grades for the task on the strength of the support they developed for their claims. The purpose of stating and supporting claims is for students to be able to analyze their original thinking about a subject as they investigate. The results of an investigation do not produce a right or wrong answer. The results of the investigation produce well-supported claims in which students have reconciled conflicting evidence and identified any errors in reasoning that may either strengthen their claims or possibly disprove their claims. Or, students must conclude that their initial claims are largely unsupported and disproven.

Begin Your Investigation Lesson With a Motivating Prompt

After you teach and model the steps of the process, begin your investigation lesson with a motivating prompt. Students will not be able to spontaneously produce claims unless you provide a prompt connected to the critical content. The provision of a well-conceived and innovative prompt will activate your students' prior knowledge and hopefully remind them of a question or intriguing idea they had during prior instruction. The prompt can be in the form of a critical question and should provide a catalyst for the investigation. This prompt may well make the difference between an effective implementation and one that never gains momentum with your students. A well-conceived prompt can keep your students engaged throughout a challenging investigation.

Provide Resources and Guidance During Investigational Tasks

Effective teachers not only check in with students frequently throughout a cognitively complex process, but they also plan ahead regarding the specifics of how and when they will provide resources and guidance along the way. A few ideas are below:

- If your students do not have prior experience identifying common logical errors, spend time modeling how to find and analyze errors in logic.

- Some teachers find it helpful to provide a template so students have structure and guidance as they learn how to investigate. Figure 1.1 provides a sample template for students to use during their investigations.

- Students can use checklists to help them organize the investigation process.

- Teachers can use peer coaching to help students check that they are on the right path. Peer coaches can vet resources, comment on the evidence supporting the resolution, and provide feedback on a draft.

Figure 1.1: Sample Template for Investigating

State a Claim (answer the question)		
What Is Known About a Subject		
Grounds #1	Grounds #2	Grounds #3
Backing	Backing	Backing
Qualifiers (confusions/ contradictions)	Qualifiers (confusions/ contradictions)	Qualifiers (confusions/ contradictions)
Conclusion (supported with grounds and backing)		

Common Mistakes

In advance of implementing this technique, teachers should consider a few of the common mistakes to avoid so their implementation can proceed more effectively:

- The teacher asks students to restate facts rather than state and support claims, thereby eliminating the opportunities for students to analyze their own thinking.

- The teacher does not expect students to support their claims with evidence.

- The teacher asks for evidence to support claims but readily accepts insufficient or incorrect evidence.

- The teacher does not require students to resolve contradictions or confusion.

- The teacher tells students how to resolve their contradictions or confusion.

Examples and Nonexamples of Investigating

The examples and nonexamples of investigating provide classroom snapshots of how teachers implement the technique in their classrooms. Although the examples may be from a different grade level or subject than you teach, view them as an opportunity to identify a new approach or an alternative way of thinking about instruction. For every example in this book, there will be a nonexample to help deepen your understanding of how and how not to implement each type of complex task. It will feature one or more of the common mistakes related to this technique to assist you in avoiding some of these errors in your implementation.

Elementary Example of Investigating

The elementary example of investigating is presented in two ways: 1) a planning template that walks you through the lesson and 2) the description of a classroom scenario based on the planning template.

Planning Template to Walk You Through the Elementary Example

Table 1.3 illustrates how an elementary science teacher completes the planning template in Table 1.2. Note that while there are multiple steps to this activity, some are brief, allowing this activity to be completed during a single class period.

Table 1.3: A Planning Template for a Fourth-Grade Science Lesson

Steps	Teacher's Notes
Identify the learning target	The learning target for this example is *obtain and combine information to describe that energy and fuels are derived from natural resources and their uses affect the environment* (NGSS 4-ESS3.1).
Determine the topic	Students will investigate the production of electricity from natural gas.
Decide on the type of investigation	This is a definitional investigation.
Identify questions or prompts	The teacher asks students to answer one of the following questions to help them state their claims: How is electricity produced from natural gas? What is the effect on the environment?
State a claim	Students state how they think electricity is produced from natural gas and the environmental effects.
Identify what is already known	Students watch videos about the production of electricity from natural gas. The students use the information in the videos to build their grounds, backing, and qualifiers.
Identify confusion or contradictions	Students watch videos produced by different sources and explain any contradictions between the videos.
Develop a plausible resolution	Students write a short summary of how electricity is produced from natural gas and the effects on the environment, making sure to resolve any contradictions.
Reflect on the initial claim	Students revisit their initial claims and state whether they are able to support their claims, using information from their summaries to explain why.

Description of a Classroom Scenario Based on the Planning Template

Students are studying how fuels are derived from natural sources and how the use of fuels affects the environment. Today's lesson focuses on the production of electricity from natural gas. To begin, the teacher asks students to do a quick write to answer the following questions:

How is electricity produced from natural gas? What is the effect on the environment?

The teacher reminds students that they should apply what they know about how coal is used to produce electricity to answer this question and that they will have an opportunity during the lesson to support the claims they make. The teacher then shows two short videos that explain how natural gas is produced. The natural gas industry produced one video, and an environmental group produced the other. The teacher gives students, who are in groups, an opportunity to summarize each of the videos and discuss the contradictions between the videos. Afterward, students write a short summary of how electricity is produced from natural gas and the effect on the environment, making sure to resolve any contradictions they noted between the videos. As the final step in the task, the students revisit their initial claims and use information from their summaries to explain how they are able to support their claims.

Elementary Nonexample of Investigating

In the nonexample classroom, the teacher provides the same prompt:

How is electricity produced from natural gas? What is the effect on the environment?

Because the videos contradict each other in some instances, the nonexample teacher decides to show only one of the videos. The teacher then leads the class in a discussion of the answers to the prompt based on the video. Students answer the prompt in their notebooks, writing a sentence or two based on a whole-class discussion of the video. The teacher does not require students to state and support individual claims. Rather than engaging in a cognitively complex task, the students in this class simply restate facts from the video.

Secondary Example of Investigating

This secondary example of investigating is presented in two ways: 1) a planning template that walks you through the lesson and 2) a description of the classroom scenario based on the planning template.

Planning Template to Walk You Through the Secondary Example

Table 1.4 describes a secondary example of an investigational task from a high school social studies lesson. As you consider this example, note that the steps are the same for a secondary historical investigation as they are for an elementary definitional investigation. The variable is the prompt you provide to students.

Table 1.4: A Planning Template for a Tenth-Grade Social Studies Lesson

Steps	Teacher's Notes
Identify the learning target	The learning target for this example is *write arguments focused on discipline-specific content. . . . Develop claim(s) and counterclaims fairly, supplying data and evidence for each while pointing out the strengths and limitations of both claim(s) and counterclaims in a discipline-appropriate form and in a manner that anticipates the audience's knowledge level and concerns* (CCSS ELA WHST 9–10.1).
Determine the topic	Students will investigate, using multiple conflicting primary sources, how conditions in the trenches influenced the daily lives of World War I (WWI) soldiers.
Decide on the type of investigation	This is a historical investigation.
Identify questions or prompts	The teacher asks the following question: *How did the conditions in the trenches influence the daily lives of WWI soldiers?*
State a claim	Students explain and give examples of how they think conditions in trenches influenced the daily lives of WWI soldiers.
Identify what is already known	Students read examples from multiple primary sources of how conditions influenced the daily lives of WWI soldiers.
Identify confusion or contradictions	Students respond to the prompt: *Find a difference between the two sources and explain that difference.*
Develop a plausible resolution	Students answer a question: *Does that make one more right than the other? Explain why. Justify your answer using details from the text.* Students analyze the information in the sources to draw conclusions about how trench warfare had an impact on soldiers' lives.
Reflect on the initial claim	Students revisit their initial claims and explain whether the evidence they compiled supports their claims.

Description of a Classroom Scenario Based on the Planning Template

A high school social studies class has been discussing causes, effects, and conditions during World War I. The teacher wants to help students understand that when information from multiple sources is contradictory, they must integrate evidence from multiple relevant historical sources and interpretations into a reasoned argument about the past based on the learning target that was previously stated.

At the end of the class on the day prior to the lesson, the teacher asks students to write a sentence or two explaining how the conditions in trenches influenced the daily lives of World War I soldiers. She explains to students that she will ask them to defend and support their statements the next day. Having begun the thinking process by stating their claims prior to the beginning of class, students can jump right into the investigation at the start of this lesson. As students walk into class, they pick up two artifacts: a letter from a soldier to his mother describing the conditions in the trenches and a picture of soldiers in the trenches. They begin by looking over the picture and annotating things they see that could help them support their claims. The teacher then has students read the letter aloud in their groups, stopping after every paragraph to discuss possible support for their claims and then jotting down notes. When students finish reading the letter, the teacher prompts them to find a difference between the two sources and explain this difference. They develop a possible resolution to the contradiction by explaining which one they believe is more correct and why, using details from the sources to justify their answers. During the last step, students individually analyze the information in the sources to conclude how trench warfare had an impact on soldiers' lives during World War I and revisit their initial claims to explain whether the evidence supports their claims.

Secondary Nonexample of Investigating

In the nonexample classroom, the teacher provides the same prompt and follows the same steps until the point in the activity at which she expects students to identify confusion or contradictions between the sources. The nonexample teacher skips this step so as not to confuse his students with sources' conflicting viewpoints. When some students point out conflicting information in the sources, the teacher tells students which one is the most reliable. The common mistake in this scenario is that the teacher does not give students opportunities to reason through what they know to decide which information to use.

Determining If Students Can Generate and Test Hypotheses Using Investigating

As your students investigate, monitor whether they are analyzing their own thinking to resolve contradictions or confusions. Build monitoring into your lesson plans from the outset. As you plan your students' investigational task, find opportunities to verify the desired result of each step of the investigation. Following are some examples of monitoring that you might use:

- Have students explain to a partner why they stated their claims, and as students are talking, walk around and listen for who is able to explain and who is not.

- Provide sticky notes for students to annotate the sources they are reading. As you circulate, read and discuss these notes with students.

- Ask students to write down the confusion or contradiction they found on the front side of an index card and the common logical error that it relates to on the back.

- Have students form groups according to the common logical error they identified and then discuss their reasoning for choosing that one. Listen to students as they discuss their rationale.

Use the student proficiency scale for investigating in Table 1.5 to help you determine if your students are demonstrating the desired results of each step. Reference it as you plan and implement investigating in your classroom.

Table 1.5: Student Proficiency Scale for Investigating

Steps for Investigating	Emerging	Fundamental	Desired Result
State a claim	Students contribute to a discussion about possible claims.	Students state a claim.	Students are able to justify their claim.
Identify what is already known	Students identify only what they have been taught about a subject.	Students identify what is known about a subject from supplemental sources.	Students build support for their claim with grounds and backing based on what is known about a subject.
Identify confusion or contradictions	Students can state that the sources do not agree on a subject, but they cannot say why they think the sources do not agree.	Students identify sources that do not agree with each other, and students identify where the confusion exists.	Students identify common logical errors that cause the confusion or contradiction.
Develop a plausible resolution	Students state a resolution.	Students develop a plausible resolution.	Students defend their resolution by stating grounds and explaining backing.
Reflect on the initial claim	Students restate their initial claim.	Students identify whether their initial claim is supported by the evidence.	Students explain why their initial claim is supported or disproven based on the resolutions they developed.

Scaffold and Extend Instruction to Meet Students' Needs

You have no doubt already identified steps in this technique that may be too difficult for some of your students if implemented exactly as they have been explained. You have also likely noted several students who are ready for more challenging versions of the technique. Use the following suggestions to inspire ideas tailored to the needs of your students.

Scaffolding

- Develop a list of potential resources available for students who do not know where to start their investigations.

- Provide possible sentence starters for students who are not yet comfortable with the language of supporting and backing a claim.

Extending

- Encourage those students who are able to quickly parse important information to rank the information in order of its strength in supporting their claims.

- Ask students who are proficient in identifying confusion or contradictions to create a step-by-step list of their thought process as they identify common logical errors that cause the confusion or contradiction. This can then help students who need support with this process.

Instructional Technique 2

PROBLEM SOLVING

While solving real-world problems can be a part of your instruction from time to time, this type of activity is *not* the same as problem solving in the context of a cognitively complex task. In this technique, students generate possible solutions to overcome an obstacle or constraint, and then test and defend their possible solutions. Conclusions are based on evidence that students document when they test their potential solutions using established criteria.

How to Effectively Implement Problem Solving

There are four steps to effectively implement problem solving with your students: 1) use the provided planning template to walk through the various steps of the problem-solving process, 2) teach and model the steps for how to solve cognitively complex problems, 3) begin your problem-solving lesson with the prompt you have chosen, and 4) provide resources and guidance during the problem-solving task.

Use the Planning Template

Carefully review the planning template shown in Table 2.1 prior to introducing this problem-solving technique to your students. Recall that while the table may appear to be a lesson plan, it is not. It is a "thinking" plan. Part 1 of the plan contains the action steps that you will take *prior* to standing in front of your students. The questions for the teacher's action steps are intended to help you identify the critical aspects of problem solving as a cognitively complex task. Note that the planning questions for problem solving differ somewhat from those you encountered in the investigation technique. However, similarly to that technique, your students will do the complex "thinking" work during this lesson. The technique will be successful only if you do *your* "thinking" homework in advance. Part 2 of the plan contains the action steps that students will follow as they predict and test a possible solution to the goal and obstacles you identified in Part 1. The planning questions in Part 2 are intended to alert you to the many decisions that must be made in advance of implementation. Part 3 includes two action steps that you will take as you monitor and observe your students engaging in their problem-solving activity.

Table 2.1: A Planning Template for Problem Solving

1. Planning Questions for Teacher's Action Steps	
Identify the learning target	With what learning target is this task aligned?
Determine a goal	What goal do you want the solution to achieve?
	Does the goal allow students to demonstrate the essential knowledge and skills of the learning goal?
Identify an obstacle	Identify an obstacle that students must overcome to achieve the goal.
	Does the obstacle allow students to demonstrate the essential knowledge and skills of the learning goal?
Provide a prompt	Use the goal and obstacle to create a prompt.
	What question will you ask to prompt the possible solution?
	Does the prompt align with the level of cognition expected in the learning target?
2. Planning Questions for Students' Action Steps	
Hypothesize a possible solution	How will you ask students to hypothesize (predict) a possible solution? (In groups? In their academic notebooks?)
Test the hypothesis	What resources will you provide?
	What parameters will you place on the testing?
	What activities might you facilitate?
	What steps will students follow to evaluate the results?
	How will students document grounds, backing, and qualifiers?
Examine the results	What steps will students follow to examine the results?
	How will students document grounds, backing, and qualifiers?
Decide if the problem is solved	What will you ask to prompt a conclusion?
	How will you ask students to support their conclusions with grounds, backing, and qualifiers?
	How will you ask students to contrast the conclusions to the initial proposed solutions?

Reflect on the process	How will you help students identify the parts of their procedure that they could improve to better test the potential solution?
	How will you help students speculate about future possible solutions based on their results?
3. Planning Questions for Teacher's Action Steps During the Implementation	
Plan to monitor	How will you check that students are analyzing their own thinking as they problem solve?
Plan to adapt	What will you plan for students who need support or extension?

Teach and Model the Steps in Problem Solving

Depending on your students and their previous experiences with structured problem solving, you may wish to teach and model the steps in this technique before expecting students to effectively use it. Teaching and modeling this process require that you walk students through each of the steps using a familiar topic, stopping to think aloud about how you tested your hypothesis, examined the results, and made the decision regarding whether your solution is supported with grounds, backing, and qualifiers. Here are the steps to include in your teaching and modeling of problem solving:

1. **Predict (hypothesize) some possible solutions for solving the problem given the stated goal and possible obstacles that must be overcome to reach that goal.**

   Before students begin the problem-solving process, select your preferred set of terms for the task: *predict* and *prediction* or *hypothesize* and *hypothesis. Predict* and *prediction* might feel like a better fit for this task in the primary grades, but think about how and when you will transition to the more formal terms *hypothesize* and *hypothesis,* since an understanding of this academic vocabulary is essential to college and career readiness.

   Give students the opportunity to brainstorm possible solutions and discuss the merits of each before asking them to settle on the possible solution they will test. When you first use the problem-solving technique, you may choose to brainstorm with the entire class or assign the brainstorming activity to small groups. Once you generate a list of possible solutions, ask students to individually pick the solution *they* think will work best. Remember, the goal of engaging students in cognitively complex tasks is to have them use content knowledge they have previously acquired to solve the problem. Be sure to explain that they will have to test and defend their solutions with solid information. If you give students your "favorite" possible solution, you deprive them of the opportunity to use their own knowledge to hypothesize a solution.

2. **Test the prediction (hypothesis).**
   Students complete the task with the obstacle (constraint) and possible solution in place. If students are unable to test their solutions in a hands-on way, suggest that they build a logical case based on facts that they collected to support or refute their possible solutions.

3. **Examine the results.**
   As students complete the testing of their predictions, they document evidence that supports or refutes their claims. Allow students time and guidance to record their findings and analyze what those findings tell them about the strength of their initial hypotheses.

4. **Decide if the problem is solved.**
   As in the other techniques described for engaging students in cognitively complex tasks, students draw conclusions based on how strongly their evidence supports or refutes their hypotheses. Students should also include qualifiers in their statements. Remind students that not all hypotheses are defensible, and even if they accurately identify what seems to them to be a defensible and logical possible solution in their hypotheses, they may sometimes discover contradictory or confusing information that casts doubt on the viability of their hypotheses. For students to state that their hypotheses can be supported, they must identify qualifiers and then explain or resolve the situations in which their possible solutions may not work.

5. **Reflect on the process.**
   Students explain how testing the potential solutions impacted their initial thinking on the topic. This metacognitive step focuses students on the depth of their own learning and helps them view themselves as successful learners. Cognitively complex tasks such as problem solving provide opportunities for students to recognize and appreciate their growing abilities to use knowledge to solve problems.

Begin Your Problem-Solving Lesson With a Motivating Prompt

The prompt you provide is the catalyst to spark the generation of a viable hypothesis followed by the testing that is needed for a successful experience. Determine the goal or desired outcome you want students to achieve. Next, create or identify obstacles or constraints that they must try to overcome to achieve the goal or desired outcome. Finally, create a prompt that requires students to analyze their own thinking about a topic to come up with a possible solution to the obstacle or constraint. Use your learning target to guide your determination of the goal, obstacle, and prompt. Remember that the goal of this cognitively complex task is to give students an opportunity to demonstrate what they understand and are able to do in relation to the learning target. Align your prompt with the cognitive complexity of the learning target.

Here are some potential prompts:

- How would you overcome . . . ?

- What solution do you think will work best?

- Develop a strategy to . . .

When students are attempting to solve a complex problem for the first time, be certain to spend time discussing the goal, obstacle, and prompt so that they understand how these work together to suggest a hypothesis. Consider developing a minilesson for students that directly teaches the meaning of the terms and provides some examples and nonexamples from familiar content.

Provide Resources and Guidance During Problem Solving

Whether you implement problem solving as a short- or long-term task, plan ahead regarding how you will support your students as they take on this challenging technique.

There are countless versions of problem and solution maps that can aid your students in the steps of problem solving. Conduct an internet search, and find one that is easily adaptable for the problem you are asking your students to solve. Before using materials that have been prepared by others, make sure they contain the essential steps of guiding your students through identifying the goal and obstacle, creating a possible solution, collecting evidence while testing the solution, and reflecting on whether their possible solution works.

Students can be great resources for each other as they engage in this process. Plan specific times and directions for how and when you want students to work together and when you want them to work independently. You might have students brainstorm possible solutions with a partner or in a small group and then individually choose the solution they would like to test. You can arrange students who selected the same possible solution to test that solution as a group, and then later require that each individual student document the evidence. Provide structure, guidance, and time limits when students are interacting with one another.

Choice helps students feel more in control and also helps students take more ownership of their learning. If possible, provide choices for your students in how they document and demonstrate their problem solving. Students might choose between showing their problem-solving steps in a slide show, poster, text, video, or other format. Whether you provide students with choices of how they can demonstrate their learning or you tell them the type of product to produce, be wary of the students who spend more time on the aesthetics of the product than demonstrating their learning. Help your students understand that their highest priority is a clear demonstration of problem solving rather than the funniest video or most colorful poster.

Common Mistakes

Here are some mistakes that teachers commonly make when initially engaging students in problem solving. Analyze the following errors in advance to help yourself implement the technique more effectively with your students:

- The teacher fails to understand that problem solving in the context of a cognitively complex task is far different from solving a real-world problem.

- The teacher provides the possible solution to be tested to the students.

- The teacher fails to expect students to contrast their hypothesized possible solutions to the results.

- The teacher fails to expect all students to provide evidence when stating their conclusions.

Examples and Nonexamples of Problem Solving

Following are two sets of examples and nonexamples, one set from elementary classrooms and a second from secondary classrooms. Recall that the classroom nonexample illustrates one or more of the common mistakes related to this technique to assist you in avoiding some of the errors.

Elementary Example of Problem Solving

The elementary example of investigating is presented in two ways: 1) a planning template that walks you through the lesson and 2) a description of the classroom scenario based on the planning template.

Planning Template to Walk You Through the Elementary Example

As you consider this elementary example of problem solving, keep in mind that each example activity is aligned with a learning target as a way for students to demonstrate their learning. Make connections between this example and the description of each step described earlier. Table 2.2 displays a planning template for a kindergarten science lesson using problem solving. Note that the upper half of the planning form consists of teacher actions before the lesson begins. The bottom half of the form consists of student actions that take place during the problem-solving activity. The shaded prompt in the middle of the form is the point at which the lesson begins. Once the example teacher has shared the prompt, the students assume responsibility for applying their previous learning to the solution of a problem.

Table 2.2: A Planning Template for a Kindergarten Science Lesson

Steps	Teacher's Notes
Identify the target	There are two learning targets for this example: *plan and conduct an investigation to compare the effects of different strengths or different directions of pushes and pulls on the motion of an object* (NGSS K-PS2-1), and *analyze data to determine if a design solution works as intended to change the speed or direction of an object with a push or a pull* (NGSS K-PS2-2).
Determine a goal	Without touching a ball after the initial push, get the ball to turn to go into a cup.
Identify an obstacle	Students cannot touch the ball after the initial push.
Provide a prompt	How can you set up an obstacle course for a ball so it will turn and go into the cup?
Hypothesize a possible solution	Students decide how and where to place objects so the ball will turn and keep moving.
Test the prediction	Students send their ball onto their course, noting if the ball turns like they thought it would.
Examine the results	Students examine the ball's movement at each part of the obstacle course to see if it does what they thought it would.
Decide if the problem is solved	Students say whether they are able to turn the ball and get it into the cup.
Reflect on the process	Students say what they would do differently next time to change the direction of the ball to get it into the cup. If they got it into the cup the first time, they can say what they would do differently if the cup were moved.

Description of the Classroom Scenario Based on the Planning Template

The example teacher introduces the activity to her kindergarten students by reviewing what they have previously discussed about how to change the speed or direction of an object by applying a push or a pull. He depicts flat obstacles facing different directions on the board and asks students to predict with their partners how each obstacle will cause the ball to change direction. He then tells students that today they will use their knowledge to get a ball to move into a cup without touching it. He explains that they will be given a ball but that they cannot touch the ball once they give it a push to start. He then shows them how the ball and cup will be arranged so that the cup is about 3 feet in front of and 2 feet to the right of the ball. The cup will be facing sideways so that it is not possible to send the ball into the cup with one push but in a way that students will need to set up only one obstacle to get the ball into the cup.

To get the students started, the teacher partners students and gives them a picture of the initial placement of the ball and the cup. He then asks them to brainstorm an answer to the following question:

How can you set up an obstacle course for a ball so it will turn and go into the cup?

He gives them time to think about and draw out possible solutions with their partner before they pick which solution they think will work best. Students also need to draw the path they think the ball will take. As the students brainstorm, he circulates, checks for accuracy, and asks students why they think their solutions will work. The teacher then has the students sit quietly on the rug while he helps the partner groups set up their chosen solution. For each trial, students watch to see if the ball goes in the cup and if the ball turns like they thought it would. After the students conduct their trial, they draw on their paper where the ball actually went. After each student group has had a turn, the teacher has each group tell another group why they think they were (or were not) able to move the ball like they thought they could to get it into the cup. They then tell classmates in the other groups how they might set up another course now that they have had the chance to rethink what they know about movement.

Elementary Nonexample of Problem Solving

The nonexample teacher takes her students through all of the steps the example teacher used. However, as she does so, instead of the students conducting the ball push, she intervenes and demonstrates each step for students. The students do not actually do any of the work. The teacher calls on students one at a time to assist her, but the majority of students are not actively participating. Therefore, most students are not required to apply what they know to solve a problem. If the teacher does all of the work, the students are deprived of opportunities to apply their own knowledge to solve a problem.

Secondary Example of Problem Solving

The secondary example of problem solving is presented in two ways: 1) a planning template to aid in the development of a lesson and 2) a description of the classroom scenario based on the planning template.

Planning Template to Walk You Through the Secondary Example

The secondary example of problem solving takes place in a seventh-grade English language arts (ELA) class. Table 2.3 contains the planning template that guides the example teacher in his lesson. Note that even though this example and the earlier elementary example have different subjects and different grade levels, the steps in the process remain the same.

Description of the Classroom Scenario Based on the Planning Template

Because the teacher has limited time in this unit, she chooses to use a cognitively complex task that, while it requires students to use their knowledge, does not require a great deal of class time. The class has been reading a story set in the 1920s, and instead of simply telling the students what details of the story align with the time period versus instances in which the author took the liberty of stretching facts to prove a point, the teacher chooses to propose a problem to her students to determine for themselves how and why the author alters history or keeps it the same in the reading. The teacher provides this prompt:

Authors of historical fiction do not specifically state which parts of the text are based on documented historical facts and which are created for the story.

- *How can a reader know what is real and what is made up?*

- *How and/or why does the author use or alter history to serve the story?*

The teacher asks students to pose answers to these questions by brainstorming before discussing their responses with their group. After students discuss their hypotheses, the teacher gives them two primary sources that contain historical accounts of the time period and asks students to note the similarities and differences between these accounts and information in the book. The students then discuss why the author may have chosen to alter historical facts within the text, and state whether they are able to tell what is real and what is made up in the story. Each student writes an analysis of whether an author's decision to stay with or stray from history serves the story. As part of their analysis, the teacher asks students to revisit their initial answer and state whether they are able to defend it or if they need to revise their thinking. Students cite evidence to support their initial hypothesis or their revision.

Table 2.3: A Planning Template for a Seventh-Grade Reading Lesson

Steps	Teacher's Notes
Identify the learning target	The learning target for this lesson is *compare and contrast a fictional portrayal of a time, place, or character and a historical account of the same period as a means of understanding how authors of fiction use or alter history* (CCSS ELA RL 7.9).
Determine a goal	Use details to compare and contrast an actual historical period with the novel and consider how and why the author alters history or keeps it the same.
Identify an obstacle	The author does not provide information to the reader on which parts of the book are based in fact and which are not.
Provide a prompt	Historical fiction authors do not specifically state which parts of the text are based on documented historical facts and which are created for the story. • How can a reader know what is real and what is made up? • How and/or why does the author use or alter history to serve the story?
Predict a possible solution	Students state how they think they can tell what is real and what is made up in the story. They also state how and why they think the author uses or alters history to serve the story.
Test the prediction	Students read historical accounts of the time period and note the similarities and differences (e.g., for events, places, and people) between these accounts and the narrative of the book.
Examine the results	Students discuss why the author may have chosen to alter historical facts within the text.
Decide if the problem is solved	Students state if they are able to tell what is real and what is made up in the story. Students each write an analysis of whether an author's decision to stay with or stray from actual facts in history serves the story.
Reflect on the process	Students revisit their initial prediction and state whether they are able to defend it or if they need to revise their thinking. Students cite evidence to support their initial prediction or their revision.

Secondary Nonexample of Problem Solving

The nonexample class has also been reading a story set in the 1920s, and the teacher also expects students to discuss how and why the author alters or keeps it the same in the reading. Because the teacher has limited time in this unit, he asks students to decide which details of the story align with the time period versus the instances in which the author takes the liberty of stretching facts to prove a point. However, the teacher does not require that his students compare the fiction with nonfiction accounts of the same time period. Without this step in his lesson, students simply state their opinions and are unable to build support with grounds and backing. Providing opportunities for students to voice their opinions has a place in the classroom, but students must understand that opinions in the context of cognitively complex tasks must be based on evidence.

Determining If Students Can Generate and Test Hypotheses From Problem Solving

Plan ahead regarding how you will check in with students during each step of this task so that you can be sure students are not getting stuck or sidetracked and are thoughtfully engaged in problem solving. Here are some options for how to monitor for the desired result during the problem-solving task:

- Have students write their possible solutions on whiteboards and hold them up for you to read. After a quick glance through the class, target those students whose possible solutions do not demonstrate an understanding of the content.

- As students are testing their hypotheses, circulate and ask them to explain to you how their evidence supports or refutes their possible solutions.

- For students to formulate their conclusions, have them highlight the key information they will use from their evidence to support their conclusions with grounds and backing. Check the highlighted information for correctness before or as students are writing their conclusions.

Use the student proficiency scale for problem solving in Table 2.4 to help you determine if your students are demonstrating the desired result of each step of the problem-solving process.

Table 2.4: Student Proficiency Scale for Problem Solving

Steps for Problem Solving	Emerging	Fundamental	Desired Result
Hypothesize a possible solution	Students can select possible solutions from a list of possible choices.	Students hypothesize possible solutions.	Students are able to explain why their possible solutions will help achieve the goal.
Test the hypothesis	Students test their hypotheses.	Students document evidence as they test their hypotheses.	Students test their hypotheses and document evidence that supports or refutes the possible solutions.
Examine the results	Students identify evidence based on the testing of their hypotheses.	Students document and analyze the evidence.	Students use evidence to build support for their possible solutions with grounds, backing, and qualifiers.
Decide if the problem is solved	Students state whether their possible solutions worked.	Students contrast results with their hypotheses.	Students contrast results with their hypotheses by supporting or refuting their claims with grounds and backing based on evidence. Students identify common logical errors that prevented the successful achievement of the goal.
Reflect on the process	Students restate their predictions.	Students identify whether their hypotheses are supported.	Students explain why their hypotheses are supported or not supported based on their conclusions.

Scaffold and Extend Instruction to Meet Students' Needs

This technique has focused on the essential components of problem solving, but only you know the needs of your individual students. You may need to adapt these steps by offering scaffolding or extending to meet their needs. Here is a list of possible ideas:

Scaffolding

- Provide a list of possible solutions for students if they are not able to generate their own ideas.

- Directly teach vocabulary and show examples and nonexamples of obstacles.

- Prepare a list of questions for students who are unable to complete the process of problem solving without support. Example questions include:

  - What do you know about the obstacle?

  - What are some ideas for overcoming the obstacle?

  - How could you test one of those ideas?

  - What evidence can you provide that your prediction is correct or not?

  - Is your possible solution working, or do you need to try something new?

  - How does your evidence support or refute your prediction?

Extending

- Encourage students who have a deep understanding of problem solving to adapt a problem-solving map so that it is more specific to their own problem.

- Allow students to create their own goal and obstacle to initiate problem solving.

Instructional Technique 3

DECISION MAKING

The decision-making process in this technique is a formal process in which students use information they have acquired from critical content to select among various possible choices. Decision-making tasks require students to predict the best alternative and then analyze their thinking to judge that alternative based on preestablished criteria to confirm or disconfirm their original hypothesis of which alternative would meet the criteria.

How to Effectively Implement Decision Making

As with the earlier techniques, there are four steps to the effective implementation of decision making in your classroom: 1) use the planning template to walk through the various steps of the decision-making process, 2) teach and model the steps for how to make decisions in the context of cognitively complex decision making, 3) begin your decision-making lesson with a motivating prompt, and 4) provide resources and guidance during the decision-making activity.

Use the Planning Template

Use the template in Table 3.1 to assist you in planning for the effective implementation of decision making in your classroom. If you already use activities that ask students to make decisions, use the template to help you adapt those tasks so that your students can attain the cognitive complexity of hypothesis generation and testing.

Table 3.1: A Planning Template for Decision Making

1. Planning Questions for Teacher's Action Steps	
Identify the learning target	With what learning target is this task aligned?
Determine a goal	What goal do you want the decision to achieve?
	Does the decision allow students to demonstrate the essential knowledge and skills of the learning target?
Develop alternatives	Will you provide the alternatives or ask students to develop their own?
	If you are providing the alternatives, identify these alternatives for students.
	Do the alternatives allow students to demonstrate the essential knowledge and skills of the learning target?
Determine criteria	Will you provide the criteria or ask students to develop their own?
	If you are providing, identify the criteria that must be satisfied to achieve the goal.
	Do the criteria allow students to demonstrate the essential knowledge and skills of the learning target?
Provide a prompt	Use the goal, alternatives, and criteria to create a prompt.
	What question will you ask to prompt the decision?
	Does it align with the level of cognitive complexity found in the learning target?
2. Planning Questions for Students' Action Steps	
Develop alternatives (the teacher can provide these)	If students are developing the alternatives, what question will you ask to elicit these alternatives?
	Will you limit the alternatives, give choices, or set parameters?
	How will you ensure the alternatives allow students to demonstrate the essential knowledge and skills of the learning target?
Determine criteria (the teacher can provide these)	If students are developing the criteria, what question will you ask to elicit criteria?
	Will you limit the number of criteria, give choice, or set parameters?
	How will you ensure the criteria allow students to demonstrate the essential knowledge and skills of the learning target?

Predict which alternative will best meet the criteria	How will you ask students to predict and share which alternative will best meet the established criteria? (In groups? In their academic notebooks?)
Evaluate the alternatives using criteria	What steps will students follow to evaluate their alternatives using the criteria? How will students document grounds, backing, and qualifiers?
Decide which alternative best meets the criteria	What questions will you ask to prompt a conclusion? How will you ask students to support their conclusions with grounds, backing, and qualifiers?
Reflect on the hypothesis	How will you ask students to reflect on how well their initial hypothesis is supported by the grounds, backing, and qualifiers?
3. Planning Questions for Teacher's Action Steps During the Activity	
Plan to monitor	How will you check that students are analyzing their own thinking as they engage in decision making?
Plan to adapt	What will you plan for students who need support or extension?

Teach and Model the Steps for Decision Making

The steps for decision making will vary depending on how comfortable your students are with the process and how complex the decision is. You will likely complete some of the steps. However, students must conduct some steps independently for them to analyze their thinking as they engage in decision making. The following steps suggest when providing guidance and information is appropriate and when students should do their own thinking:

1. **Predict which alternative will best meet the criteria.**

   Present the alternatives and criteria to your students, or have them develop their own. Ask them to hypothesize which of the alternatives they think will best satisfy the criteria. Students will then focus on confirming or disconfirming their hypotheses. A student discussion about the hypotheses will provide an opportunity for you to determine that students do indeed understand the range of alternatives and can specifically explain what each alternative entails.

2. **Evaluate the alternatives using the criteria.**

   The key to decision making is that students are able to evaluate all of the alternatives specifically against each criterion. Some students will want to look at the criteria more holistically, but in doing this they run the risk of missing the critical attributes of one or more criteria. This is the step in the process during which students establish grounds, backing, and qualifiers. Therefore, they must document their findings so they are prepared to defend their decisions. Use a decision-making matrix such as the one in Figure 3.1 to help students organize their thoughts during this step, especially during their initial encounter with the decision-making process.

3. **Decide which alternative best meets the criteria.**

    Based on their evaluation of the alternatives against the criteria, students determine which alternative meets the greatest number of the identified criteria. Students should use their documented grounds, backing, and qualifiers from the previous step. Help your students understand that they need to do more than simply identify the best alternative; they need to justify their decision using the evidence they collected. If the evaluation of the alternatives does not provide a clear preferred choice, students can add criteria to help them make a decision.

4. **Reflect on the predicted choice.**

    Students justify how they have confirmed or disconfirmed their initial prediction based on their evaluation of alternatives. To do this, students decide if their predictions are confirmed because the selected alternative meets most of the criteria or other alternatives meet more criteria and therefore are shown to meet the criteria more completely than the one they hypothesized.

Figure 3.1: Sample Template for Decision Making

What is the decision you are making?	
Alternatives: A. B. C. D. E.	**Criteria:** 1. 2. 3. 4. 5.

Predict which alternative you think will best meet the criteria and explain your thinking:

Criteria	Alternative A	Alternative B	Alternative C	Alternative D	Alternative E
1.					
2.					
3.					
4.					
5.					

Notes and evidence:

Decision and justification:

Reflection:

Begin Your Decision-Making Lesson With a Motivating Prompt

Decision-making tasks require the construction of a scenario about which students need to make a decision that will demonstrate their mastery of the learning target. To create such a scenario, first think of the goal you want your students to achieve. What do you want them to decide? Next, determine if you will provide the alternatives for students to choose between, if they will develop their own, or if a combination of both would be most suitable. The next step is to develop criteria. Criteria are the standards by which the alternatives will be judged when making the decision. As with developing alternatives, the students can determine the criteria or you can identify some and have the students add to the list. Last, ask a question that focuses your students on the decision they need to make. Here are some potential prompts:

- Which among the following would be best?

- What is the best way to . . . ?

- Which of these is most suitable?

Provide Resources and Guidance During Decision Making

You know your students and the experience they bring to this technique. Use this information to plan ahead for the resources and guidance they may need to be successful in their decision-making experience. As your students become more comfortable with cognitively complex tasks, their needs will change. Following is a list of possible ways to support students. Revisit these suggestions each time you tackle a new decision-making process.

- When students are learning how to be thoughtful and deliberate in their decision-making process, it can be helpful to provide them with the following list of steps:

  1. Identify the goal (this is an interpretation of the teacher's prompt).

  2. Identify the alternatives.

  3. Predict the alternative you think will satisfy the most criteria.

  4. Generate the criteria that will determine the alternative you choose.

  5. Weigh the criteria to consider whether certain criteria hold more weight or are more important than others.

6. Evaluate or rank your alternatives in terms of how they satisfy the criteria.

7. Decide which alternative best meets the criteria.

8. Revisit your hypothesis, and explain how the alternative you selected meets the criteria most completely.

- Encourage students to use their academic notebook or previous work to develop alternatives, write their hypotheses, or determine criteria. This exercise will help them see the connection between what they have previously learned and this activity.

Common Mistakes

No one likes to make mistakes, especially when they can be prevented with forethought and preparation. Awareness of potential mistakes teachers make when implementing decision making can help you avoid them. Plan ahead to avoid these more common mistakes:

- The prompt does not require students to evaluate alternatives using criteria to make a decision.

- The activity includes too many alternatives or criteria for students to successfully evaluate.

- The teacher, instead of the students, evaluates the criteria.

- The teacher tells students how their evaluation supports or refutes their initial decision.

Examples and Nonexamples of Decision Making

As you consider the following examples and nonexamples of implementing decision-making tasks in your classroom, note ways you can effectively implement the technique and consider how to avoid the mistakes in the nonexamples.

Elementary Example of Decision Making

This elementary example of decision making is set forth in two ways: 1) a planning template that walks you through the lesson and 2) a description of the classroom scenario based on the planning template.

Planning Template to Walk You Through the Elementary Example

As you consider this elementary classroom example of decision making, keep in mind that it is aligned with two learning targets as a way for students to demonstrate their learning in the content area of mathematics. Table 3.2 displays a planning template for this fifth-grade lesson using decision making. As in previous techniques, the top half of the planning form consists of teacher actions that take place before the lesson formally begins. The bottom half of the form consists of student actions that take place during the decision-making activity. The shaded prompt in the middle of the form is the point at which the lesson begins. Once the teacher shares the prompt, the students assume responsibility for applying their previous learning to the decision-making process.

Table 3.2: A Planning Template for a Fifth-Grade Math Lesson

Steps	Teacher's Notes
Identify the learning targets	This example is based on two learning targets: *convert among different-sized standard measurement units within a given measurement system (e.g., convert 5 cm to 0.05 m), and use these conversions in solving multi-step, real world problems* (CCSS Math 5.MD.1), and a*pply the formulas V = l × w × h and V = b × h for rectangular prisms to find volumes of right rectangular prisms with whole number edge lengths in the context of solving real world and mathematical problems* (CCSS Math 5.MD.5.b).
Determine a goal	Students will decide which package meets the criteria of being the lightest box with the largest volume.
Develop alternatives	There are four packages with varying measurements to compare.
Determine criteria	The package that meets the most criteria will cost the least to send: ● has the least mass ● has the largest volume
Provide a prompt	Your dad wants to ship a fragile object to your sister in another country. He can package it in one of four boxes. He wants to know which box will hold the most and has the least mass, since that will be the least expensive to ship and will allow the most protective wrapping. He left you the measurements, and you need to convert them so you can help him decide which box has the largest volume and the least mass.
Predict which alternative will best meet the criteria	Students hypothesize: ● Which package do you think will satisfy the criteria, costing the least to send? Explain why to your neighbor.
Evaluate the alternatives using criteria	Students answer the question: How can you prove this? Develop a plan for how to compare the measurements so you know which box meets the criteria.
Decide which alternative meets the criteria	Based on the evaluation, students decide which meets the criteria.
Reflect on the hypothesis	Students state whether their hypotheses are supported or not and why.

Description of the Classroom Scenario Based on the Planning Template

The teacher spends the beginning of class reviewing conversion and volume with her students. The activity for today calls for students to use the knowledge they have acquired to make a decision as to which measurements are greatest. She provides the prompt:

Your dad wants to ship a fragile object to your sister in another country. He can package it in one of four boxes. He wants to know which box will hold the most and has the least mass, since that will be the least expensive to ship and will allow the most protective wrapping. He hands you the measurements, and you need to convert them so you can help him decide which box has the largest volume and the least mass.

She gives them the following table of measurements:

Box	A	B	C	D
Mass	0.4 kg	500 g	8 hg	25 dag
Side lengths	35 cm	0.5 m	5.5 dm	400 mm
	x 45 cm	x 0.3 m	x 8 dm	x 200 mm
	x 55 cm	x 0.1 m	x 6 dm	x 90 mm
Volume				

The teacher asks the students:

Which box do you think will meet the criteria and therefore cost the least to send? Explain why to your neighbor.

They are given time in their groups to develop a plan for how to compare the measurements to know which box meets the criteria. Students convert the measurements and compare them to see which box has the least mass and largest volume.

The teacher has the conversions prepped and ready to check against her students' answers.

Answers

	A	B	C	D
Mass	400 g	500 g	**800 g**	250 g
Side lengths	0.35 m	0.5 m	**0.55 m**	0.4 m
	× 0.45 m	× 0.3 m	**× 0.8 m**	× 0.2 m
	× 0.55 m	× 0.1 m	**× 0.6 m**	× 0.09 m
Volume	0.87 m³	0.015 m³	**0.264 m³**	0.0072 m³

After the students show which box meets the criteria by converting the measurements to a common unit, the teacher asks them to state whether their original hypothesis is proven or not and why.

Elementary Nonexample of Decision Making

The nonexample teacher simply provides the prompt and has students make the decision without first asking them to hypothesize or use the formal process to make the decision. Without the hypothesis, students do not have an opportunity to go back to their original thinking to see whether their hypothesized decisions are correct. Remember that the point of hypothesis generation and testing is that students analyze their own thinking as they use their knowledge. If they simply convert the measurements, they do not have an opportunity to realize they used their decision-making ability in a real-life situation to confirm or disconfirm their hypotheses.

Secondary Example of Decision Making

The secondary example of decision making is presented in two ways: 1) a planning template that walks you through the lesson and 2) a description of the classroom scenario based on the template.

Planning Template to Walk You Through the Secondary Example

The secondary example of decision making takes place in a seventh-grade ELA class. Table 3.3 contains a planning template that summarizes the teacher's lesson plan. Note that the lesson begins when the teacher presents a prompt.

Table 3.3: A Planning Template for a Seventh-Grade Reading Lesson

Steps	Teacher's Notes
Identify the learning target	The learning target for this example is *compare and contrast a written story, drama, or poem to its audio, filmed, staged, or multimedia version, analyzing the effects of techniques unique to each medium, for example, lighting, sound, color, or camera focus and angles in a film* (CCSS ELA RL 7.7).
Determine a goal	Decide which poetry reading best conveys the meaning of the poem.
Develop alternatives	Multiple audio/filmed renditions of the same poem.
Determine criteria	Teacher provides the criteria: • The reader uses intonation and inflection to convey meaning. • The audio techniques (volume, background music) enhance the meaning of the poem. • The video techniques (lighting, color, camera angle) enhance the meaning of the poem.
Provide a prompt	Poetic readers make decisions about how to present a poem. Analyze readings of the same poem to decide which reader influences the listener or viewer more.
Predict which alternative will best meet the criteria	Students listen to a description of the readings and state the one they feel will best influence the listener or viewer.
Evaluate the alternative using criteria	Students evaluate all alternatives and cite examples of how the work meets each of the criteria.
Decide which alternative will best meet the criteria	Based on the evaluation, students decide which reading satisfied the criteria most effectively.
Reflect on the predicted choice	Students state whether their original hypotheses meet the criteria

Description of the Classroom Scenario Based on the Planning Template

For students to analyze the effects of techniques unique to the various media, the teacher creates a task that will involve students in decision making about which of a number of poetry readings best conveys the meaning of the poem. To do that, he presents audio, filmed, and multimedia renditions of the same poem and provides the following prompt:

Poetic readers make decisions about how to present a poem.

Analyze readings of the same poem to decide which reader influences the listener or viewer more.

Before students begin listening to or viewing the renditions, the teacher gives some background information about each of the renditions and then provides students with the criteria to guide their decision making:

- The reader uses intonation and inflection to convey meaning.

- The audio techniques (volume, background music) enhance the meaning of the poem.

- The video techniques (lighting, color, camera angle) enhance the meaning of the poem.

The students listen to or view each of the renditions once and then talk with their partners about which rendition they think will meet the most criteria and therefore influence the listener more readily. The teacher wants them to consider the criteria more carefully, so he has the students then listen to or view each of the renditions again and make notes about how well the rendition meets the criteria using specific examples in their notes. Afterward, students decide which reading is most effective based on their evaluations, citing examples of how each rendition meets each of the criteria. Last, they state whether their original hypotheses are confirmed or not and why.

Secondary Nonexample of Decision Making

The nonexample teacher outlines the same steps for his students but gives students the freedom to select their own poem. After explaining the steps, the teacher allows several days for the students to complete the activity, including researching and finding a poem with multiple renditions. Throughout the day the teacher circulates and answers questions as they arise. He checks in with students to make sure they are on task. It becomes apparent that some students are quickly able to find a few renditions of the poem they picked and others have not been able to select a poem after a significant amount of time. The teacher does not have a backup poem for those students, so he tells them that they need to come to class the next day with a poem selected. The next day, some students still do not have a poem with multiple renditions. The teacher then has to decide if he will allow extra time, take in work regardless of how much some students have completed, or allow students to complete the assignment with what they have. Choice is good, but not when it becomes the focal point of the activity. This teacher could have allowed students to select among a few poems he knew had multiple renditions or set a specific time limit for research with a backup poem for those who had not found their own in that preset time limit.

Determining If Students Can Generate and Test Hypotheses Using Decision Making

Monitoring whether students are able to confirm or disconfirm their hypotheses with grounds, backing, and qualifiers is quite straightforward. If your students are working together, walk around and listen to them discuss the alternatives and criteria. Look over their shoulders as they document their evidence. Interact with them, asking questions and listening, to ensure they are not just engaged, but they are actively analyzing their thinking to make a decision. Some teachers carry around a pad of sticky notes to document students who need more follow-up. If you want to make sure you are checking in with all students, carry a class roster and make your notes on a clipboard. Think about how you can ask your students to quickly demonstrate the desired result of each step. They can answer questions on mini-whiteboards or as exit passes, allowing you quick checks that students are effectively analyzing their thinking.

- Why do you predict that alternative to be the best?

- How are the criteria helping you select among the alternatives?

- Do the results fit with your original prediction? If not, how has your thinking changed?

- How does this task allow you to demonstrate where you are on the student proficiency scale?

The desired results of each step of decision making, as well as levels of proficiency leading up to the desired results, are in Table 3.4. Review it as you plan and implement decision making in your class.

Table 3.4: Student Proficiency Scale for Decision Making

Steps for Investigating	Emerging	Fundamental	Desired Result
Develop alternatives	Students read the alternatives the teacher provides.	Students develop or can identify the alternatives.	Students develop the alternatives and describe why the alternatives are plausible.
Determine criteria	Students read the criteria the teacher provides.	Students determine or identify the criteria.	Students determine the criteria and explain how the criteria will help them make a decision.
Predict which alternative will best meet the criteria	Students contribute to a discussion about a possible hypothesis.	Students hypothesize which alternative will best meet the criteria.	Students are able to justify their hypotheses.
Evaluate the alternatives using criteria	Students evaluate the alternatives.	Students evaluate the alternatives using criteria.	Students document grounds, backing, and qualifiers for their initial decision as they evaluate the alternatives.
Decide which alternative best meets the criteria	Students make a hypothesis that an alternative meets the criteria.	Students evaluate the alternatives using criteria.	Students explain which alternative best meets the criteria.
Reflect on the hypothesis	Students restate their hypotheses.	Students identify if their hypotheses are confirmed or disconfirmed.	Students explain why their hypotheses are confirmed or disconfirmed based on their evaluation of alternatives and how poorly the other alternatives are supported.

Scaffold and Extend Instruction to Meet Students' Needs

Your students seldom arrive in your classroom with the same experiences or background knowledge. Some students need scaffolding to utilize their knowledge in decision-making tasks. Other students need their learning extended beyond the planned decision-making task to grow. The following suggestions are examples to help you tailor this task to the precise needs of your students.

Scaffolding

- In advance, think about what questions you would ask a student who is struggling. Have that list ready for selected students who are unable to move forward without your probing questions. This could assist them in getting unstuck, and you will then be free to move about, checking in with other students.

- If students are struggling with evaluating the alternatives, they may lack a clear understanding of the alternatives and/or criteria. Determine if they understand by asking them to describe each alternative and criterion to a partner or you.

- Form a small group and conduct a minilesson reteaching the meanings of difficult terms as well as providing familiar examples and nonexamples.

Extending

- Some students may prefer to make their own graphic organizer rather than use the one provided. If students are proficient with the steps of decision making, allow them choices as long as they include the required steps.

- If some students are more comfortable using technology to organize their thoughts, give them the opportunity to use the platform they prefer to work in, if possible.

Instructional Technique 4

EXPERIMENTAL INQUIRY

Many teachers of subjects other than science may be tempted to skip over experimental inquiry as a teaching technique, thinking it does not relate to their content. In reality, however, teachers can use experimental inquiry with virtually any content. The defining attribute of experimental inquiry is that students collect evidence by direct observation to test a hypothesis they have generated. This can occur in many ways, including reading a text, watching a video, feeling or observing a physical change, and listening to an interview or sounds of an instrument. The College and Career Readiness Anchor Standards for Writing state that students must be able to effectively select, organize, and analyze content. Experimental inquiry is the process of doing just that. Whether it is content in a book or data in a lab, the inquiry process is about knowing when and how to select, organize, and analyze evidence of any kind.

The experimental inquiry technique differs from the investigating technique in that students design the procedure they will use for collecting evidence, whereas in the investigating technique, the teacher assigns a specific investigation procedure to students.

Experimental inquiries originate when students observe something they are unable to explain and want to investigate it further (Marzano & Heflebower, 2012). The heart of experimental inquiry is that students—not teachers—determine or design the procedure they will use to test their hypotheses. Students use their initial observations to formulate hypotheses and then create procedures to test the validity of their hypotheses.

How to Effectively Implement Experimental Inquiry

There are five aspects of effectively implementing experimental inquiry with your students: 1) use the planning template to walk through the various steps of the experimental inquiry process, 2) teach and model the steps for how to generate a hypothesis and test it, 3) set up a demonstration for your students and describe for them what you observe happening, 4) begin your experimental inquiry lesson with the prompt you have identified, and 5) provide resources and guidance during the experimental inquiry task.

Use the Planning Template to Master the Steps of the Experimental Inquiry Process

Use the template in Table 4.1 to guide your planning. Each step has questions that can help you identify the type of direction and assistance you might give students to better ensure a successful inquiry experience for them. Note how this planning template differs from earlier templates in two ways. First, overall, there are fewer action steps for you to implement. Second, you are expected to release more responsibility to students for thinking and planning in an experimental inquiry. Therefore, once you identify the learning target with which the task will be aligned, your second "action" step requires that you *set up a demonstration*. You will then use your demonstration to create a prompt that will guide students to design procedures to support their hypotheses.

Table 4.1: A Planning Template for Experimental Inquiry

1. Planning Questions for Teacher's Action Steps	
Identify the learning target	With what learning target is this task aligned?
Set up a demonstration	About what topic do you want students to inquire?
	Does it align with the topic of the learning target?
	What demonstration will you provide to prompt the experimental inquiry?
	How will you ask students to document their description of the demonstration?
Use your demonstration to create a prompt	What question will you ask to prompt the experimental inquiry?
	Does it align with the level of cognition of the learning target?

2. Planning Questions for Students' Action Steps	
Generate a hypothesis	How will you ask students to answer the question? (In groups? In their academic notebooks?)
Design a procedure to test the hypothesis	How will you help students connect what they have observed to their experimental design?
	What materials will students need to carry out their procedure?
	How will you check the design before the implementation?
Implement the procedure	What resources will you provide?
	What parameters do you want in place?
	What activities might you facilitate?
Examine the results	What steps will students follow to examine the results?
	How will students document grounds, backing, and qualifiers?
Evaluate the results	What will you ask to prompt a conclusion?
	How will you ask students to support their conclusions with grounds, backing, and qualifiers?
Reflect on the process	How will you ask students to contrast their conclusions to the initial prediction?
	How will you help students identify parts of their experimental design that could improve to better test their hypotheses?
	How will you help students wonder about future hypotheses and inquiries based on their results?
3. Planning Questions for Teacher's Action Steps at the Close of the Activity	
Plan to monitor	How will you check that students are analyzing their own thinking as they engage in experimental inquiry?
Plan to adapt	What will you plan for students who need support or extension?

Set Up a Demonstration or Observation for Students

One of the ways that experimental inquiry differs from the other techniques is that it begins with a demonstration or observation to spark students' hypotheses. This demonstration should intrigue your students and lead them to generate a hypothesis they will test through experimental inquiry. Think about what you can demonstrate and have students observe that will align with the learning target and lead students to hypotheses. As students observe, they should describe what they see so they are actively participating in this step. Their descriptions will also help them justify their hypotheses.

Use the Results of Your Demonstration and Description to Generate a Prompt

The purpose of the demonstration or observation is to prompt students to inquire further to better understand what they observed. Students will base their hypotheses and subsequent procedures on the demonstration or observations you provide. Try the following sample prompts for your experimental inquiry:

- How would you test that . . . ?

- How would you determine if . . . ?

- How can this be explained?

1. **Generate a hypothesis.**
   Students generate a hypothesis regarding what they think they will discover in their inquiry and the thought processes that lead them to it. This step drives the design of their procedures since the point of the experimental inquiry is to prove or disprove hypotheses. Provide students with adequate time to think about some possible options for a hypothesis before asking them to choose one. Then, guide them to justify or explain the reasoning behind their hypotheses. This process will help students take ownership of the inquiry from the beginning.

2. **Design a procedure to test the hypothesis.**
   Students create the procedure they will use to test the hypothesis. Some examples of ways students can collect data to support or refute their hypotheses include questionnaires, interviews, observations, experiments, surveys, and various resource texts. Even though students are developing the actual procedures they will follow, set parameters for their procedures to ensure the safety of students and any individuals they may include in their procedures. Students must seek teacher approval before beginning any experimental inquiry. Not only does this step ensure safety, but it also identifies any students whose initial procedures are flawed.

3. **Implement the procedure.**
   Students implement the procedures they designed. The structure and guidance you provide is essential in this step because you may have students conducting multiple procedures simultaneously. Assist students with troubleshooting their procedures as needed and do not hesitate to check in with them frequently. Occasionally remind them

to maintain a lively pace as they conduct their inquiries. You may find it helpful to have students work in small groups for this step.

4. **Examine the results.**
   This step will occur in conjunction with the previous step as students document their findings to build support for their hypotheses. With multiple ongoing procedures, there will be various types of data being organized and summarized. Monitor to ensure that students are organizing and summarizing their data.

5. **Evaluate the results.**
   To conclude their experimental inquiry, students state their hypotheses and explain how the evidence they collected when they implemented the procedure supports or refutes it. Ensure that students have adequately summarized the data rather than merely presented it as recorded and represented.

6. **Reflect on the process.**
   Students explain how the inquiry has an impact on their initial thinking on the topic. During this step, expect students to examine their own content learning and describe how this process added to or changed their prior thinking. This type of metacognitive processing helps students view themselves as learners and increases their ability to self-manage cognitively complex tasks.

Provide Resources and Guidance During Experimental Inquiry

Develop a set of resources or supplies in advance of introducing the experimental inquiry. If students request other supplies or resources and they are available, add them to your list; however, do not feel obliged to provide everything students might need. The key to managing the variety of inquiries and student needs in the experimental inquiry is a concept called *bounded choice*. Bounded choice means that you provide students with a limited number of choices as well as setting boundaries or limits to the inquiry in the interest of logistics and safety.

A graphic organizer that depicts the steps of experimental inquiry can be useful to students. Remember that completing the steps so they can use their knowledge and analyze their thinking is more important than memorizing the steps of the process. Figure 4.1 is a template you can use to guide students in the experimental inquiry process.

Figure 4.1: Sample Template for Experimental Inquiry

The question I am investigating is . . .	Based on my current knowledge, I think . . .

To test this theory, I will . . .

As a result of this, I found out . . .

Grounds	Backing	Qualifiers

Therefore . . .

Common Mistakes

As you begin to implement experimental inquiry in your classroom, be aware of potential mistakes. Here are some of the more common ones:

- The teacher provides the hypothesis for the students to test.

- Students know the results they are supposed to get in advance of the inquiry.

- The teacher suggests or mandates a certain procedure to students.

- Students are allowed to implement a procedure that will not give viable results.

- Students do not document their evidence as they conduct the inquiry.

- Students are not expected to support or refute their hypotheses using evidence collected in the inquiry.

- One student in a group does the work, and the others copy.

Examples and Nonexamples of Experimental Inquiry

As you consider the following examples and nonexamples of implementing experimental inquiry in classrooms, be aware of how the example teachers effectively implement the technique, and note the common mistakes the nonexample teachers make.

Elementary Example of Experimental Inquiry

The elementary example of experimental inquiry is presented in two ways: 1) a planning template that walks you through the lesson and 2) a description of the classroom scenario based on the planning template.

Planning Template to Walk You Through the Elementary Example

This elementary example describes an experimental inquiry in a first-grade math class. As one part of their morning work, small groups of students rotate through this inquiry at a station. Table 4.2 describes the lesson steps and is followed by a classroom scenario.

Table 4.2: A Planning Template for a First-Grade Math Lesson

Steps	Teacher's Notes
Identify the learning target	The learning targets for this example are *order three objects by length; compare the lengths of two objects indirectly by using a third object* (CCSS Math 1.MD.1), and *express the length of an object as a whole number of length units, by laying multiple copies of a shorter object (the length unit) end to end; understand that the length measurement of an object is the number of same-size length units that span it with no gaps or overlaps. Limit to contexts where the object being measured is spanned by a whole number of length units with no gaps or overlaps* (CCSS-Math-1.MD.2).
Set up a demonstration or a description	Point out two features of the classroom that are located in different places (e.g., the bottom of the door and the side of the teacher's desk). Also, give each group a piece of string equal to the distance between the bottom of the door and the side of the teacher's desk. Ask students to describe how the length of the objects (door, desk, string) are the same and how they are different.
Use observation to create a prompt	Ask students to order the desk, door, and string from shortest to longest.
Generate a hypothesis	Students order the three objects from what they think is the shortest to the longest.
Design a procedure to test the prediction	Ask students: *How can you find out whether you're right? Make a plan to check that you are correct.*
Implement the procedure	Students use the string to measure the door and the desk. This will allow them to compare all three objects.
Examine the results	Students write down if the string is longer or shorter than the door and the desk.
Evaluate the results	Ask students to order the length of the objects based on what they found by measuring.
Reflect on the process	Students revisit their order and state whether they are correct. Students say what else they could use this process to order the length of.

Description of the Classroom Scenario Based on the Planning Template

The teacher has been working with her class on measurement, and it is now time for the students to use the knowledge they have gained so they can order three objects by length and compare the lengths of two objects indirectly by using a third object. Knowing that some of her students are stronger readers than others, she puts the students in groups of three today, making sure that at least one student will be able to understand and explain the directions. At the station she has set up, students find a piece of string that is of a length in between that of the bottom of the door and that of the side of the teacher's desk and receive the following prompt:

Order the desk, the door, and the string from shortest to longest.

The teacher knows that some students will probably not understand the sentence, so she has included pictures of the three objects and labeled the side of the teacher's desk and the bottom of the door with big arrows so students know what to measure when it is time. Students then label the pictures of the desk, the door, and the string with 1, 2, and 3 in the order they think is correct. Below that, students are asked to make a prediction:

How can you find out if you are right? Make a plan to check that you are correct.

This time the teacher knows that pictures will not be enough to ensure they are on the right track, so she has students check in with her before moving forward with their plans. This way, she gives students time to brainstorm and plan without having to catch them at just the right moment. But this also means that she has to make herself available when each group is ready to discuss their plan and guide them as necessary. Since she knows how important this step is, she has made sure that students can work independently at the other stations. Planning ahead will free her up to assist students with this cognitively complex task. After the teacher approves each plan, the students measure the door and the desk. She then asks them to order the objects once again based on the string measurements. The final question at the station asks students to reflect:

Was your order correct?

Are there other things in the room that you can compare the length of using the same method?

The students know that they can draw their answer if they are not able to write it, and the teacher will ask them any clarifying questions needed to understand their thinking.

Elementary Nonexample of Experimental Inquiry

In this nonexample, a first-grade teacher realizes that some of her students will not be able to figure out how to compare the lengths. Planning ahead, the teacher decides to circumvent this problem by telling students the steps they need to take to measure the desk and the door by using the string. This shortcut deprives her students of the opportunity to individually reason about how to compare the length of two objects by using a third object. Some students will discern from the activity how to use this information in other situations, but for other students, the only lesson they may learn is how to measure using a piece of string since they did not have the opportunity to use their own knowledge to design the procedure.

Secondary Example of Experimental Inquiry

This secondary example of experimental inquiry is presented in two ways: 1) a planning template that walks you through the lesson and 2) a description of the classroom scenario based on the planning template.

Planning Template to Walk You Through the Secondary Example

The steps for a secondary science example for experimental inquiry are in Table 4.3. Notice that this is not a typical science experiment. In this example, students use observations to hypothesize categories of plant structures and then develop a plan to test their hypotheses.

Table 4.3: A Planning Template for a Middle School Science Lesson

Steps	Teacher's Notes
Identify the learning target	The learning target of this example is *use an argument based on empirical evidence and scientific reasoning to support an explanation for how characteristic animal behaviors and specialized plant structures affect the probability of successful reproduction of animals and plants respectively* (NGSS MS-LS1-4).
Set up a demonstration or observation	Show several examples of reproductive structures of plants (hard nuts, bright flowers, pollen from trees, seeds with wings). Students describe the general features of each reproductive structure on paper and to their partners.
Use the demonstration to create a prompt	Ask students: *Now that you have looked at all of the structures, categorize the structures according to the ways they help plants reproduce. Remember that there is not just one way to categorize them, but make sure you are thinking about plant reproduction when you make your categories.*
Generate a hypothesis	Students hypothesize different categories for the structures. Categories can include before and after pollination, animal or environmental assistance, and so on.
Design a procedure to test the hypothesis	Ask students: *How can you make sure that your categorization makes sense? Make a plan to check that you are correct.*
Implement the procedure	Students use their textbooks or other resources to examine how specialized plant structures affect the probability of successful reproduction.
Examine the results	Students document the information that supports or refutes their categories.
Evaluate the results	Students explain how specialized plant structures affect the probability of successful reproduction.
Reflect on the process	Students revisit their initial categories and state whether they are able to defend them or they need to revise their thinking. Students cite evidence to support their initial prediction or their revision. Students also state how they could use these categories to determine how plant structures they encounter in the future aid in reproduction.

Description of the Classroom Scenario Based on the Planning Template

Following is a descriptive scenario showing how a teacher implements the lesson in a single middle school class period:

Before class, the teacher writes the learning target on the board: *explain how specialized plant structures affect the probability of successful reproduction.*

When the students walk into class, they find examples of various reproductive structures of plants (hard nuts, bright flowers, pollen from trees, seeds with wings, etc.) at each lab table and a graphic organizer on which they are expected to record the general features of each reproductive structure. After a few minutes, they are asked to discuss their answers with their partners. The teacher walks around reading the responses, listening to the partners discuss, and prompting students to think about how these structures assist reproduction.

The teacher then prompts the students to generate hypotheses:

Now that you have examined all of the structures, categorize how these structures affect the probability of successful reproduction. Remember that there is no one way to categorize them, but make sure when you select your categories you are thinking about how each structure affects the probability of successful reproduction.

The teacher has students work with their partners to categorize the structures in an organization of their choosing. For example, categories might include before and after pollination or animal or environmental assistance.

The teacher then prompts students to investigate their hypotheses:

How can you determine if your categorization is accurate?

Students throw out many ideas, both productive and unproductive. The teacher then asks students to spend two minutes with their partners planning how they will test the validity of their categorization. Because time and resources are limited, the teacher puts constraints on the investigation, limiting the students to the print resources they have in class, which include the textbook and a selection of library books the teacher provided.

Students spend time looking up and documenting the information that supports or refutes their categories. If students find their categories are incorrect, the teacher encourages them to revise their initial categories based on their new thinking. Knowing that some students will struggle to find evidence, the teacher has sections in some books tabbed so that she can quickly refer students to specific text if they need support in that way. She also provides blank graphic organizers, such as tables and web diagrams, for students who want or need extra structure for their categorization.

After students determine whether their hypotheses are supportable, the teacher asks each student to explain in a paragraph how specialized plant structures affect the probability of successful reproduction by revisiting initial categories and stating whether they are able to defend them or they need to revise their thinking. She tells students to cite evidence to support their initial hypotheses or their revision.

Secondary Nonexample of Experimental Inquiry

In the nonexample classroom, the teacher tells students how to categorize the plant structures and then has students explain how each of the structures belongs in the category into which the teacher placed it. In this scenario, the students do not have opportunities to create their own categories. They are merely supporting the teacher's claim, not generating their own hypotheses.

Determining If Students Can Generate and Test Hypotheses From Experimental Inquiry

Before students implement their procedures, ask them to get approval from you. This not only ensures that students will be safe and successful, but also it allows you to discuss the reasoning for the procedures they designed.

As students are implementing their procedures, walk around and read over their shoulders to ensure they are documenting evidence they can later use for grounds, backing, and qualifiers.

Feedback strips, as shown in Figure 4.2, are a useful way to monitor your students' ability to analyze their thinking. You will not likely use feedback strips with all students. Select one or two students who need special attention. As students are engaged in the inquiry, note where they fall on the scale and provide them a quick note of support.

Figure 4.2: Feedback Strips for Experimental Inquiry

How well did you . . . **observe and describe**?	Students see the content but do not make observations.	Students make observations about the content.	Students can explain how the observations prompt the experimental inquiry.
Notes			

How well did you . . . **make a prediction**?	Students contribute to a discussion about possible predictions.	Students make a prediction.	Students are able to justify their prediction.
Notes			

How well did you . . . **design a procedure to test the prediction**?	Students plan a procedure.	Students design a procedure to test the prediction.	Students can explain how their procedure will allow them to test the prediction.
Notes			

How well did you . . . **implement the procedure**?	Students implement a procedure.	Students implement the procedure as it was designed.	Students document evidence that supports or refutes their predictions as they implement the designed procedure.
Notes			

(continued on next page)

Figure 4.2: Feedback Strips for Experimental Inquiry (continued)

How well did you . . . **examine the results?**	Students identify evidence based on the procedure.	Students document evidence they observe as they implement the procedure.	Students use evidence they observe to build support for their predictions with grounds, backing, and qualifiers.
Notes			

How well did you . . . **evaluate the results?**	Students state their conclusions.	Students explain their conclusions.	Students defend their conclusions with grounds, backing, and qualifiers.
Notes			

How well did you . . . **reflect on the process?**	Students restate their predictions.	Students identify whether their predictions are correct or incorrect.	Students explain why their predictions are correct or incorrect based on their conclusions.
Notes			

Table 4.4 provides a student proficiency scale for experimental inquiry. The scale can help you determine if your students are demonstrating the desired result of each step. With this information, you can pinpoint the feedback you give to maximize their success.

Table 4.4: Student Proficiency Scale for Experimental Inquiry

Steps for Experimental Inquiry	Emerging	Fundamental	Desired Result
Describe the demonstration or observation	Students witness the demonstration or observation but do not describe it.	Students describe what they observe.	Students can explain how their observations helped them create their hypotheses.
Generate a hypothesis	Students contribute to a discussion about possible hypotheses.	Students hypothesize based on their observations.	Students are able to justify their hypotheses.
Design a procedure to test the hypothesis	Students implement a procedure.	Students implement the procedure as it is designed.	Students document evidence that supports or refutes their hypotheses.
Implement the procedure	Students implement a procedure.	Students implement the procedure as it is designed.	Students document evidence that supports or refutes their hypotheses as they implement the designed procedure.
Examine the results	Students identify evidence based on the procedure.	Students document evidence they observe as they implement the procedure.	Students use evidence they observe to build support for their hypotheses.
Evaluate the results	Students state a conclusion.	Students explain their conclusions.	Students defend their conclusions with evidence.
Reflect on the process	Students restate their hypotheses.	Students identify if their hypotheses are confirmed or disconfirmed.	Students explain how their hypotheses are confirmed or disconfirmed based on their conclusions.

Scaffold and Extend Instruction to Meet Students' Needs

As you implement more experimental inquiries in your classroom, you will become more skilled at identifying and adapting for the needs of your students. In the beginning, plan ahead to anticipate and adapt for those needs. To do that, you might ask for assistance from a coach or mentor. Here are some examples of how you can provide support or extensions as students conduct experimental inquiries.

Scaffolding

- If students are unable to design their own procedure, have them sort example procedures into categories of *plausible* and *nonplausible*. They can then use the plausible ones to create their own or use one provided.

- Allow students who get stuck to go on a "walkabout" where they look at other students' work and get ideas for their own.

Extending

- Have students describe how they would design their procedures differently if they conducted the same inquiry again.

- Ask students to come up with another conclusion using the same evidence, and then compare the grounds, backing, and qualifiers for each conclusion to determine which is the best.

Instructional Technique 5

INVENTING

Inventing, at first glance, may appear to be something reserved for robotics class or woodworking, but in actuality, students invent or create all the time. You probably have more than one activity already in your repertoire that has the markings of inventing. Inventing is similar to problem solving, but has the express purpose of creating and testing a prototype (trial product) to meet criteria. Prototypes come in many forms, including an advertisement, a painting, a new game, and a Rube Goldberg machine, to name a few.

For this technique, students analyze their own thinking as they brainstorm how to design something that achieves a specific goal, select the design they think will meet the criteria, and then build or create a prototype. After the prototype is operational, students test, evaluate, and troubleshoot it based on preestablished criteria to prove their invention achieves the goal.

How to Effectively Implement Inventing

There are four steps to effectively implementing inventing: 1) use the planning template to walk through the various steps of the inventing process, 2) teach and model the steps for how to generate and test hypotheses as they apply to the inventing process, 3) begin your inventing lesson with the prompt you have chosen, and 4) provide resources and guidance during the design and construction of a prototype.

Planning to Implement Inventing in Your Classroom

The following planning template (Table 5.1) contains the steps and questions you must address as you plan to implement inventing for the first time.

Table 5.1: A Planning Template for Inventing

Steps	Planning Questions
Identify the learning target	With what learning target is this task aligned?
Determine a goal	What goal do you want the prototype to achieve? Does the goal for the prototype allow students to demonstrate the essential knowledge and skills of the learning goal?
Determine criteria	Identify the criteria the prototype must meet to achieve the goal. Does the criteria for the prototype allow students to demonstrate the essential knowledge and skills of the learning goal?
Provide a prompt	Use the goal and criteria to create a prompt. What question will you ask to prompt the design of the prototype? Does it align with the level of cognition of the learning target?
Brainstorm ideas	Will you limit the number of ideas, give choice, or set parameters? How will you ensure the ideas allow students to demonstrate the essential knowledge and skills of the learning goal?
Design a prototype	How will you connect the design process to the criteria? What materials can students use to design the prototype? How will you ask students to design? (In groups? In their academic notebooks?) How will you check the design before beginning the building process?
Build the prototype	What resources or materials will you provide? What parameters will you place on the building process? What activities might you facilitate?
Evaluate the prototype using criteria	What steps will students follow to evaluate the prototype? How will students document grounds, backing, and qualifiers?
Revise the prototype	How will students decide if they need to revise their design? What additional guidance will you provide those who do? What will you expect of a revision?

Explain how the prototype achieves the goal	What will you ask to prompt a conclusion?
	How will you ask students to support their conclusions with grounds, backing, and qualifiers?
Reflect on the design	How will you ask students to contrast their conclusions to the initial designs?
	How will you help students identify parts of their designs that could improve to better demonstrate the criteria of the goal?
Plan to monitor	How will you check that students are analyzing their own thinking as they invent?
Plan to adapt	What will you plan for students who need support or extension?

Teach and Model the Steps of the Inventing Process

Your decision regarding when and how to teach and model the steps of the inventing process will depend on your grade level, content, and students. However, inventing is a complex and multifaceted technique, and teaching and modeling the steps for your students will be beneficial to both you and them. Only when you begin to unpack the various aspects of this technique will the common mistakes and need for more planning before implementation become evident. Students will need a working knowledge of the vocabulary and its meaning in the context of inventing. They will also benefit from seeing how you personally construct a prototype using the steps they will follow once you begin implementation with them.

Use your learning target to help you decide what your students might invent to demonstrate essential knowledge and skills. Develop a few options in advance so that as you create your prompt and facilitate students' brainstorming, you will have a general direction in mind to guide your students. Note that not all learning targets lend themselves to all cognitively complex tasks. To ask students to invent, the learning target must lend itself to this technique. Following are the steps students will follow as they design and build their prototypes.

1. **Brainstorm ideas.**

    Students create a list of ideas to meet the criteria. Have students brainstorm multiple possibilities, select the one they think will best meet the criteria of achieving the goal, and explain why they think so. Remember that in the beginning you may need to guide students more, but you want them to decide which idea they think will be the most viable.

2. **Design a prototype.**

   The prototype can be a new product or it can be an improvement on an existing product. Have students draw and describe what they plan to build before they build it. Your students might find it helpful if you build in feedback and editing steps before they create or build their prototypes. This can help ensure a greater chance of success. Because this feedback is focused on how well the prototype meets the criteria, if you provide guiding questions, students can give each other feedback, freeing you up to check for accuracy and assist students who need it.

3. **Build the prototype.**

   Students create or build their prototypes based on their designs. Think ahead of time of possibilities so you can plan for questions students might have as they build. The prototypes do not need to be elaborate; they simply need to meet the criteria. Helping students stay focused on that can be tricky at times but will be worth it when you see how successful they can be when they keep learning in mind.

4. **Evaluate the prototype using criteria.**

   Students should then judge their completed prototypes against the criteria you provided. If the prototypes were built to perform a task, students should test their performance. Students love seeing how their prototypes fare against each other and the criteria when put to the test. Remember that the purpose of this step is for students to build grounds, backing, and qualifiers for their claims by documenting evidence of how well the prototypes meet the criteria, which means you may need to remind students about the importance of having evidence when it comes time for them to explain how their prototypes achieve the goal.

5. **Revise the prototype (if necessary).**

   Hopefully any big missteps get corrected during the design phase of inventing, but if the invention does not achieve the goal, the student should back up to the design phase to improve, rebuild, and retest. Helping students understand that this is a normal part of inventing is key.

6. **Explain how the prototype achieves the goal.**

   At the conclusion of this task, students explain whether their prototypes achieved the goal using evidence they documented during the evaluation of the prototypes. Their conclusions should describe how the original prototype is successful or whether they need to revise it to successfully meet the criteria.

7. **Reflect on the design.**

   Students reflect on the design and explain how they would redesign their prototypes if they were to create or build another version. Students might engage in this type of reflection even if their own design meets all the criteria. The purpose of this step is to help students realize how their thinking changes in the course of the invention process. Help students understand that even though they might have created something that meets the criteria, they have likely learned a great deal more about the topic and can use this knowledge to further enhance their designs.

Begin the Inventing Lesson With the Prompt You Have Chosen

As with the other techniques, once you thoroughly understand the technique based on a close reading of the planning template and teach and model the process for students, your next step is to create a prompt that entices students to generate and test a hypothesis related to designing and building a prototype. In the course of reviewing the planning template and modeling the process for students, you have likely identified the goal you want students to achieve and compiled a draft of some basic criteria against which students will evaluate their prototypes. The criteria should lead students to demonstrate essential knowledge and skills. Students can determine the criteria, or you can identify an initial set and have students add to the list as needed. Be sure to have students describe and define the criteria before using them to ensure they understand how to apply that knowledge. Following are some possible prompts to inspire and motivate your students to invent.

- Create something that will . . .

- What could you build to . . . ?

- How could you . . . ?

Provide Resources and Guidance During the Inventing Process

The goal of this technique is that students will have opportunities to design, create, and test a prototype to demonstrate essential knowledge and skills. Computer design programs and elaborate art projects should not be substituted for the cognitively complex task of inventing. Structure and guidance can ensure that any potential time wasters are eliminated at the outset. Set guidelines for the amount of time spent on each phase, including designing, building, and testing. Have parameters for, or provide, the materials students can use to design and build. Provide ongoing feedback to students. Acknowledge your students' efforts about what is going well, and then offer insights and direction to those who need it.

Peer response groups can help focus your students' work. Students can share their designs and elicit peer feedback. Provide guiding questions or protocols to support students if they are uncomfortable with peer feedback.

Self-reflection can also help students remain focused on the essential knowledge and skills. Have students specifically identify how their designs demonstrates the learning target or level of performance on a scale. Then ask them what they could change or add to their designs to move to the next level of the scale.

Common Mistakes

Following is a list of the more common mistakes that teachers sometimes make when implementing this technique:

- The teacher does not establish a meaningful goal or criteria but simply directs students to create something.

- The teacher does not allow students to develop their own designs, thereby depriving them of opportunities to brainstorm and learn from other students.

- The teacher provides the prototype for the students to test.

- The teacher does not expect students to refine their design or prototype even though it does not meet the criteria.

- The teacher does not ask the students to provide evidence when stating their conclusions.

- The teacher does not expect students to reflect on the results.

Examples and Nonexamples of Inventing

Following are two sets of examples and nonexamples, one from an elementary classroom and the other from a secondary classroom.

Elementary Example of Inventing

The elementary example of inventing is presented in two ways: 1) a planning template that walks you through the lesson and 2) the description of a classroom scenario based on the planning template.

Planning Template to Walk You Through the Elementary Example

The planning template in Table 5.2 illustrates the steps for implementing the inventing technique in an elementary ELA classroom.

Table 5.2: A Planning Template for a Third-Grade Reading Class

Steps	Teacher's Notes
Identify the learning target	The learning target for this example is *use text features and search tools (e.g., key words, sidebars, hyperlinks) to locate information relevant to a given topic efficiently* (CCSS-ELA-RI3.5). Note: The learning target for this example goes beyond the above standard because students actually create their own text features, which is an extension of this standard.
Determine a goal	Create a text feature to be used with a selection of text.
Develop criteria	Provide criteria for students. The text feature • is chosen based on the type of information in it • includes information from the text • clarifies the text
Provide a prompt	Create a prompt. *The text features from your passage have been removed. Predict one text feature the author might have used to enhance understanding of your passage. Sketch these features.*
Brainstorm ideas	Students read the passage, look through the list of possible text features, and decide which one they think will work best for their passage.
Design a prototype	Students sketch their text features and then share the sketches and passage with another group to gain feedback.
Build the prototype	Students use the feedback to make final revisions to their drawings.
Evaluate the prototype using criteria	Students are asked to • explain how that text feature is the most appropriate one for the passage • highlight the information in the passage that is in the text feature • explain what the text feature is saying
Revise the prototype	If students find their prototypes do not match the criteria, they revise their prototypes.
Explain how the prototype achieved the goal	Students explain how the text features correspond with and clarify the passage.

Reflect on the design	Students answer questions and compare their final products with the text features the author uses.
	Did your group correctly identify the text features the author uses? If not, how do your and the author's text features contribute to understanding in similar and different ways?

Description of the Classroom Scenario Based on the Planning Template

The class has learned to identify and use many different types of text features, and now the teacher wants her students use their knowledge to create text features that correspond with selected texts. She prepares for the lesson by removing the text features from selected passages and then groups students according to reading ability. To start the lesson, the teacher hands out the passages to the student groups and asks them to read it, look through a list of text features they have learned, and decide which one they think will work best for their passage. To make that decision, the teacher reminds students of the criteria for text features:

The text feature

- is chosen based on the type of information in it

- includes information from the text

- clarifies the text

After all student groups hypothesize which text feature they think should be used for their passage, they sketch the text feature and then share the sketches and passage with another group to gain feedback. Students then use the peer feedback to make final revisions to their drawings. After they revise their text features, the teacher asks students to evaluate the prototype:

- Explain how a particular text feature is the most appropriate one for the passage.

- Highlight the information in the passage that is part of the text feature.

- Explain what the text feature is saying.

If students realize their text features do not match the criteria, they revise. The teacher then asks students to write a sentence or two explaining how their text features correspond with and clarify the passage. Finally, the teacher shows students the text feature that was originally used with the passage and asks them to discuss with their group the following questions:

> *Compare your text feature with the one the author uses. Did your group correctly identify the text features the author uses? If not, how do your and the author's text features contribute to understanding in similar and different ways?*

Elementary Nonexample of Inventing

The teacher provides the prompt and allows students time to brainstorm ideas for which text feature to create. The students then create the text feature and turn it in. The teacher realizes that several students have created a text feature that does not fit with or clarify the text and assigns grades to these students accordingly. In this classroom, the teacher does not give students an opportunity to get feedback and revise their original idea. The purpose of inventing is for students to use their knowledge to create something; part of that process is analyzing and revising both their thinking and the product when necessary. If the teacher skips this step, students may never revise their original thinking even though the teacher corrects the assignment.

Secondary Example of Inventing

The secondary example of inventing is presented in two ways: 1) a planning template that walks you through the lesson and 2) a description of the classroom scenario based on the planning template.

Planning Template to Walk You Through the Secondary Example

Table 5.3 contains a planning template for implementing the cognitively complex task of inventing in a seventh-grade math class.

Table 5.3: A Planning Template for a Seventh-Grade Math Lesson

Steps	Teacher's Notes
Identify the learning target	The learning target for this example is *solve real-world and mathematical problems involving area, volume, and surface area of two- and three-dimensional objects composed of triangles, quadrilaterals, polygons, cubes, and right prisms* (CCSS-Math-7.G.6).
Determine a goal	Create a math game in which participants solve word problems and equations for area, surface area, and volume.
Develop criteria	The following criteria are provided for students: The game features word problems and equations for students to solve for ● area ● surface area ● volume
Create a prompt	Create a math game in which participants solve word problems and equations for area, surface area, and volume.
Brainstorm ideas	Students brainstorm word problems and equations for a game.
Design a prototype	Students make word problems and equations they can include in their game and get feedback from their peers as to whether the problems meet the criteria.
Build the prototype	Students use the feedback to make their game.
Evaluate the prototype using criteria	The teacher asks students to state how the word problems and equations in the game meet the criteria.
Revise the prototype	If students find the word problems and equations in their game do not meet the criteria, they revise their game.
Explain how the prototype achieved the goal	Students explain how the game asks participants to solve word problems and equations involving area, surface area, and volume.
Reflect on the design	Students answer questions: *Did you have to redesign any part of your game? How did the redesign better achieve the criteria? How could you change the game to more effectively help players solve word problems and equations involving area, surface area, and volume?*

Description of the Classroom Scenario Based on the Planning Template

The example teacher wants to create a culminating activity for the unit in which students solve word problems and equations involving area, surface area, and volume. The teacher has students brainstorm ideas and sample problems for a game with a partner. She stresses that the purpose of the game is to solve word problems and equations involving area, surface area, and volume, so students who focus on fun twists and coordinating colors will not fare as well on the assignment as students whose game may not be as flashy but meets the criteria.

She gives them time to create the sample problems for their games. When they finish, the teacher groups each pair with another pair to get feedback from their peers as to whether the problems meet the criteria. After the pairs accept or reject the sample problems and give feedback on how to enhance the games, students use the feedback to make their games. The teacher then gives students time to revise any problems that did not meet the criteria and work on their games. When students turn in their games, the teacher requires them to also turn in a paragraph with the following questions answered:

- How do the problems in the game meet the criteria?

- Did you have to redesign any part of your game?

- How did the redesign better achieve the criteria?

- How could you change the game to more effectively help players solve problems involving area, surface area, and volume?

Secondary Nonexample of Inventing

The teacher asks students to create a game at the end of the unit on area, surface area, and volume. The teacher does not provide criteria to the students for what expectations the game should meet. As a result, some students focus on only one of the three topics. The teacher then does not know whether students are able to create and solve problems related to the other two topics. Outlining the criteria ahead of time not only helps students analyze their thinking, but it also helps the teacher and students focus on what is important in this activity.

Determining If Students Can Generate and Test Hypotheses From Inventing

Ahead of your implementation, plan the activities you will use to monitor your students' ability to generate and test hypotheses during the process of inventing. Following are ways to monitor to assess your students' abilities to grapple with cognitively complex tasks in the context of inventing:

- Have students number each of the criteria and then number the part of their designs that correlates to the specific criteria.

- As students test their prototypes, ask them to underline the grounds, circle the backing, and put a box around the qualifiers. Circulate the classroom, checking not only that students are completing the task but also that the information they are recording is accurate.

- Use self-reflection strips to check in with your students. Figure 5.1 contains a variety of strips you can use at different times during the inventing process.

Figure 5.1: Sample Self-Reflection Strips for Inventing

Name _____   To improve my design, I would like to learn more about . . .   To learn more, I will . . .

Name _____   The prototype I designed will achieve the goal because . . .   Changes I could make to the design before I build the prototype include . . .

Use the student proficiency scale in Table 5.4 to help you monitor and give feedback to your students on their ability to demonstrate the desired result of each successive step.

Table 5.4: Student Proficiency Scale for Inventing

Steps for Inventing	Emerging	Fundamental	Desired Result
Brainstorm ideas	Students read the ideas the teacher provides.	Students develop or can identify the ideas for the prototype.	Students can describe how the ideas meet the criteria.
Design a prototype	Students can identify a design that might work.	Students design a prototype that meets the criteria.	Students are able to explain why their designs addresses the criteria to achieve the goal.
Build the prototype	Students build prototypes.	Students build prototypes based on their designs.	Students can explain how their prototypes are based on their designs to meet the criteria.
Evaluate the prototype using criteria	Students test the prototypes.	Students test their prototypes against the criteria.	Students are able to explain why their prototypes meet the criteria to achieve the goal.
Revise the prototype	Students revise their prototypes.	Students revise their prototypes based on the evidence.	Students can explain why their revisions should better address the criteria to achieve the goal.
Explain how the prototype achieved the goal	Students state whether their prototypes achieved the goal.	Students explain how their prototypes achieved the goal.	Students support or refute their initial designs with grounds and backing based on evidence of how well their prototypes achieve the goal. Students identify pitfalls along the way.
Reflect on the design	Students describe their designs.	Students identify whether their designs meet the criteria.	Students explain why their hypotheses are proved or disproved based on their conclusions.

Scaffold and Extend Instruction to Meet Students' Needs

There will always be students who do not fit into the lesson plan you have created. For those students, it is important to determine what part of the planned activity might not work for them and then plan for options accordingly. Here are some ideas to get you started.

Scaffolding

- If some students become frustrated during the planning phase, give them opportunities to walk around and observe how other students are overcoming the obstacles they encounter.

- Provide an outline for students to follow to support their conclusions with grounds, backing, and qualifiers.

Extending

- Some students may respond well to having more criteria. The extra challenge may help them think about the essential knowledge and skills from a more unique perspective.

- Students may benefit from revising their designs and re-creating their prototypes to address the criteria more completely, even if their first test achieves the goal.

Instructional Technique 6

STUDENT-DESIGNED TASKS

As your students grow their independence as learners, consider asking some or even all of them to design their own cognitively complex tasks. This can heighten their sense of motivation and efficacy as learners, and it is the logical culminating activity for developing students who are prepared for the academic challenges of college and career.

In this technique, students design their own tasks. They decide what their focus will be and have freedom to pursue specialized interests. For student-designed tasks to be successful, students need a firm grasp regarding how to conduct a cognitively complex task since they will assume the responsibility for designing and conducting it independently. You can implement this technique with students who quickly grasp the mechanics of hypothesis generation and testing and are ready for an extension, or as a culminating task at the end of a unit or year in which you have taught, modeled, and provided support to help your students master the earlier techniques in the book.

If you are just beginning to implement cognitively complex tasks, allowing students to create their own task may not feel comfortable. Do not think you need to allow students complete choice in the beginning. The other, more structured techniques for engaging in cognitively complex tasks are very beneficial. Once you become more at ease with the process of students generating and testing hypotheses, think about how you can slowly open up choice. Start by setting parameters, and make sure you check with students as they determine the best type of task to test the hypotheses. When you move to this stage of implementation, you also might think about introducing this to a few students who need extension opportunities rather than to the entire class.

How to Effectively Implement Student-Designed Tasks

As with most of the other techniques, there are four steps to the effective imple-mentation of student-designed tasks in your classroom: 1) use the planning template to prepare to implement student-designed tasks, 2) teach and model the steps for students to design their own task, 3) begin the task by providing a prompt that allows students the opportunity to design their own task, and 4) provide resources and guidance as students design and complete the task.

Use the Planning Template

When implementing student-designed tasks, use the planning template in Table 6.1 to walk through the process before you implement the technique in your classroom. Although this template is divided into three sections, much like the templates in other techniques, it differs somewhat since students will be responsible for selecting the type of task they will use. The planning tem-plates from other techniques will likely be helpful to students for review.

Teach and Model the Steps for Student-Designed Tasks

The second step for effectively implementing student-designed tasks is teaching and modeling the steps. Once you teach and model the two steps for designing a task, students can follow the steps they have already learned for the specific task type they choose.

1. **Answer the prompt.**
   Students will use the information they already learned and the learn-ing targets for the lesson to answer one of the questions based on their own interests. Emphasize and demonstrate that the topic they choose for their task needs to align with a learning target.

2. **Implement the appropriate cognitively complex task.**
   Help your students understand that based on the topic they select, they will likely find that one type of task better allows them to suffi-ciently explore the answer to the question. For instance, if they choose to answer the question about a decision they would like to explore, that lends itself to the decision-making task.

Table 6.1: A Planning Template for Student-Designed Tasks

1. Planning Questions for Teacher's Action Steps	
Identify the learning target	With what learning target is this task aligned?
Provide a prompt	What question will you ask to prompt the task?
	Does the prompt align with the level of cognition of the learning target?
2. Planning Questions for Students' Action Steps	
Answer the prompt	How will you ask students to answer the question? (In groups? In their academic notebooks?)
	Will you limit the number of ideas, give choice, or set parameters?
Accomplish the task	How will you ensure the task allows students to demonstrate the essential knowledge and skills of the learning target?
	What resources will you provide?
	How will you organize the students to conduct the task?
	How will you check that students have included the necessary steps in their tasks?
3. Planning Questions for Teacher's Action Steps During the Activity	
Plan to monitor	How will you check that your students are analyzing their own thinking as they design and conduct their own tasks?
Plan to adapt	What will you plan for students who need support or extension?

Begin Your Student-Designed Task Lesson With a Motivating Prompt

For students to design their own cognitively complex task to generate and test a hypothesis, a prompt is needed to initiate a hypothesis. This question or statement focuses students on a topic of personal interest related to the learning target. Prompts can come from any of the other techniques and will help shape the type of task the student creates. Here are sample prompts that focus students on the various techniques:

- What are your initial questions and predictions about information we have been studying? How could you test this hypothesis?

- Is there a particular experiment you would like to conduct using the information we have been studying?

- Is there a particular problem you would like to examine using the information we have been studying?

- Is there a particular decision you would like to examine using the information we have been studying?

- Is there a particular concept you would like to investigate using the information we have been studying?

- Is there a particular invention you would like to create using the information we have been studying? (Marzano, 2007)

Remember that the purpose of this technique is that students will demonstrate what they understand and are able to do related to the learning target. Alignment to the level of cognitive complexity of the learning target can be difficult to plan for when starting out, but selecting the appropriate learning target is essential to making this final technique a meaningful learning experience.

Provide Resources and Guidance During Student-Designed Tasks

Throughout this process, frequently check that students are moving steadily in the right direction. Content knowledge can be strengthened only if students are implementing a process that will enable them to test their hypotheses.

- Setting timelines and intermediate goals can help students remain focused, even during short-term tasks. For example, if you predict the task will take just thirty minutes to complete, outline for students what you expect them to accomplish in the first ten minutes, the second ten minutes, and so on. Time structures will remind students that every minute matters and will break the task into manageable chunks.

- Peer coaching, when done correctly, enhances student learning during the development process of the student-designed task. Peer response groups can be used to share drafts of a student's plan to stimulate feedback and coaching advice on strengths and weaknesses of the plan. Students can also ask guiding questions to help their partners think through supporting their conclusions with grounds, backing, and qualifiers. If this is new to students, provide questions or sentence stems.

- Provide opportunities for metacognition to allow students to think about themselves as learners. Students can reflect on why they are learning and identify any barriers that impede their learning.

- Facilitate small-group or individual student discussions related to how students are progressing toward their learning goals while they perform their tasks.

Common Mistakes

Once you have successfully facilitated other types of cognitively complex tasks, you are ready to grant students more choice and autonomy. Before you begin, consider this list of common mistakes to ensure that your implementation is as powerful as it can be:

- The teacher tells students the topic.

- The teacher does not ask students to generate and test a hypothesis.

- The teacher does not align the task with the level of cognitive complexity of the learning target.

- The teacher does not give the students the opportunity and support to deviate from specific steps.

Examples and Nonexamples of Student-Designed Tasks

The examples and nonexamples of student-designed tasks are different from those in the earlier techniques. There are two basic steps, with the remaining steps being adapted from earlier techniques, as students design their own tasks.

Elementary Example of Student-Designed Tasks

The elementary example of student-designed tasks is presented in two ways: 1) a planning template that walks you through the lesson and 2) the description of a classroom scenario based on the planning template.

Planning Template to Walk You Through the Elementary Example

Table 6.2 illustrates how a fourth-grade social studies teacher completes the planning template described earlier in Table 6.1.

Table 6.2: A Planning Template for a Fourth-Grade Social Studies Lesson

Steps	Teacher's Notes
Identify the learning target	There are two learning targets for this elementary example: *identify a region in New York State by describing a characteristic that places within it have in common, and then compare it to other regions* (New York Grade 4 Comparison and Contextualization), and *use location terms and geographic representations, such as maps, photographs, satellite images, and models, to describe where places are in relation to each other, to describe connections between places, and to evaluate the benefits of particular places for purposeful activities* (New York Grade 4 Geographic Reasoning).
Provide a prompt	*Is there a geographic representation (map, photos, satellite images, models) you would like to create to describe characteristics of a region of New York?*
Answer the prompt	Students choose which region of New York they want to focus on, then decide which type of geographic representation will help them best describe the characteristics of that region.
Conduct the task	Students follow the steps of inventing to complete this task.

Description of the Classroom Scenario Based on the Planning Template

In this elementary classroom, the teacher is focused on two learning targets from the social studies standards. To begin the lesson, the teacher prompts the students:

> *Is there a geographic representation (map, photos, satellite images, models) you would like to create to describe characteristics of a region of New York?*

The students first pick the region of New York they want to focus on. They then gather in small groups to brainstorm with other students who have chosen the same region. Their brainstorming goal is to figure out the type of geographic representation they think will help them best describe the characteristics of that region.

The teacher reminds students that they just invented a cognitively complex task using inventing from their previous unit, and she reviews the steps of that technique with them.

The students work to create their geographic representations using the implementation steps of inventing in Instructional Technique 5, while the teacher walks around asking guiding questions and providing support and resources as necessary.

Elementary Nonexample of Student-Designed Tasks

The nonexample teacher is using the same learning targets and begins his lesson this way:

> *Is there a geographic representation (map, photos, satellite images, models) you would like to create to describe characteristics of a region of New York?*

As the students are thinking about their answers, the teacher shows students several maps from previous classes and encourages students to draw a map since that task is more straightforward and less time consuming.

The nonexample teacher makes the common mistake of taking the decisions out of the students' hands for what to do and how to do it, thereby losing all of the benefits of the technique.

Secondary Example of Student-Designed Tasks

The secondary example of student-designed tasks is presented in two formats: 1) a planning template that walks you through the lesson and 2) a description of the classroom scenario based on the planning template.

Planning Template to Walk You Through the Secondary Example

Table 6.3 illustrates how a seventh-grade social studies teacher combines two learning targets to motivate her students to design a task.

Table 6.3: A Planning Template for a Seventh-Grade Social Studies Lesson

Steps	Teacher's Notes
Identify the learning target	The learning targets for this example are *with some guidance and support from peers and adults, develop and strengthen writing as needed by planning, revising, editing, rewriting, or trying a new approach, focusing on how well purpose and audience have been addressed* (CCSS-WHST-6–8.5), and *identify ways the United States works with other nations through international organizations, such as the United Nations, Peace Corps, and World Health Organization* (Florida-SS.7.C.4.2).
Provide a prompt	*Is there a particular concept you would like to investigate using the information we have been studying?*
Answer the prompt	Students discuss with a partner whether they want to focus on the United Nations, Peace Corps, or World Health Organization. They then choose a topic to investigate further.
Conduct the task	Students follow the steps of investigating to complete this task.

Description of the Classroom Scenario Based on the Planning Template

The teacher starts with the prompt:

Is there a particular concept you would like to investigate using the information we have been studying?

Students discuss with a partner whether they want to focus on the United Nations, Peace Corps, or World Health Organization. They then choose a topic to investigate further. Different students choose different topics. The teacher listens as students discuss to ensure that their topics are aligned with the learning target:

Identify ways the United States works with other nations through international organizations, such as the United Nations, the Peace Corps, and the World Health Organization.

The teacher then reminds students that they have conducted many investigations before and that this one should follow the same process. Students use their academic notebooks to follow the investigation steps previously recorded to obtain information and begin their writing.

As the students conduct their investigation, the teacher walks around asking clarifying questions and providing support when needed.

Secondary Nonexample of Student-Designed Tasks

The nonexample teacher provides the same prompt and has students create their responses based on what they have already learned in class. The teacher allows students to use their notes and other resources to build their cases. When the students are done, they turn them in.

The teacher makes the mistake of not asking students to generate and test a hypothesis. Without asking students to plan and reflect, they miss out on the all-important opportunity to analyze how their thinking grows through this process.

Determining If Students Can Design Their Own Tasks

The purpose of monitoring is to ensure that you know which students can successfully analyze their thinking and which students need more support or extending. Here are suggestions you can use to monitor that your students are able to analyze their own thinking to design a task:

1. Ask students to do a quick write on their reasons for picking the topic they chose, so you can read over their shoulders and determine whether they are able to explain why they are designing their particular task.

2. If the task is a long-term one, taking multiple days to complete, use an approach such as the "Please look at . . . " sticky notes. Students write "Please look at . . . " and then fill in the blank to focus your feedback. This allows you to monitor and give feedback without having to digest every aspect of the task.

3. Ask students to reflect on what they have learned as they conducted this task and how it helped them demonstrate the learning target. You can assign this as an exit ticket that you can read after class or walk around looking over students' shoulders to read your students' responses.

The student proficiency scale in Table 6.4 is designed to help you determine if your students are demonstrating the desired results of each step.

Table 6.4: Student Proficiency Scale for Student-Designed Tasks

Steps for Student-Designed Tasks	Emerging	Fundamental	Desired Result
Answer the prompt	Students contribute to a discussion about possible topics.	Students state their topics.	Students are able to explain why they chose their topics.
Conduct the task	Use the student proficiency scale for the specific technique that students design to know whether students are successfully completing the task.		

Scaffold and Extend to Meet Students' Needs

As you are monitoring that your students can design their own tasks, you will most likely realize that some students are quickly able to create their own tasks, while other students struggle each step of the way. In either case, they can benefit from adaptations. If students are stuck, extra scaffolding may be necessary; if the task does not challenge students, an extension may be necessary. Here are some ideas for both scaffolding and extending.

Scaffolding

- If students are struggling with generating their own tasks, give them several options from which to choose.

- Allow periodic opportunities for students to see and hear what classmates are doing and how they are testing their hypotheses.

Extending

- If students quickly grasp how to create their own tasks, have them create step-by-step directions for the tasks explaining their thought processes for each step.

- As students complete their tasks, ask them to compare and contrast with someone else their techniques for generating and testing hypotheses, focusing on their reasons for selecting a particular hypothesis.

Conclusion

The goal of this guide is to enable teachers to become more effective in helping their students *analyze their own thinking and utilize their knowledge by generating and testing hypotheses.*

To determine if this goal has been met, you will need to gather information from your students, as well as solicit feedback from your supervisor or colleagues, to find someone willing to embark on this learning journey with you. Engage in a meaningful self-reflection on your use of the strategy. If you acquire nothing else from this book, let it be the *importance of monitoring.* The tipping point in your level of expertise and your students' achievement is *monitoring.* Implementing this strategy well is not enough. Your goal is the desired result: evidence that your students have developed a deeper understanding of the content by *engaging in cognitively complex tasks.*

To be most effective, view implementation as a three-step process:

1. Implement the strategy using your energy and creativity to adopt and adapt the various techniques in this guide. In this case, engage students in cognitively complex tasks that require hypothesis generation and testing such that students analyze their own thinking in the process.

2. Monitor for the desired result. In other words, while you are implementing the technique, determine whether that technique is effective with your students. Check with students in real time to immediately see and hear that they are able to analyze their own thinking as they generate and test hypotheses.

3. If, as a result of your monitoring, you realize that your instruction was not adequate for students to achieve the desired result, seek out ways to change and adapt.

Although you can certainly experience this guide and gain expertise independently, the process will be more beneficial if you read and work through its contents with colleagues.

Reflection and Discussion Questions

Use the following reflection and discussion questions during a team meeting or even as food for thought prior to a meeting with your coach, mentor, or supervisor:

1. How has your instruction changed as a result of reading and implementing the instructional techniques found in this book?

2. What ways have you found to modify and enhance the instructional techniques found in this book to scaffold and extend your instruction?

3. What was your biggest challenge, in terms of implementing the instructional strategy?

4. How would you describe the changes in your students' learning that have occurred as a result of implementing this instructional strategy?

5. What will you do to share what you have learned with colleagues at your grade level or in your department?

References

Achieve, Inc. (2015). *Next Generation Science Standards: For states, by states*. Washington, DC: National Academies Press. Retrieved January 11, 2015, from http://www.nextgenscience.org/next-generation-science-standards

Common Core State Standards Initiative. (2010). *Common Core state standards for English language arts & literacy in history/social studies, science, and technical subjects*. Washington, DC: Author. Retrieved September 23, 2011, from http://corestandards.org/assets/CCSSI_ELA%20Standards.pdf

Davies, A. (2007). *Making classroom assessment work*. Courtenay, BC, Canada: Connected Publishing.

Dickson, S. V., Collins, V. L., Simmons, D. C., & Kame'enui, E. J. (1998). Metacognitive strategies: Instructional and curricular basics and implications. In D. C. Simmons & E. J. Kame'enui (Eds.), *What reading research tells us about children with diverse learning needs* (pp. 361–380). Hillsdale, NJ: Erlbaum.

Dougherty, E. (2012). *Assignments matter: Making the connections that help students meet standards*. Alexandria, VA: Association for Supervision and Curriculum Development.

Fisher, D., & Frey, N. (2007). *Checking for understanding: Formative assessment techniques for your classroom*. Alexandria, VA: Association for Supervision and Curriculum Development.

Flach, T. (2011). *Engaging students through performance assessment: Creating performance tasks to monitor student learning*. Englewood, CO: Lead+Learn Press.

Marzano, R. J. (2007). *The art and science of teaching*. Alexandria, VA: Association for Supervision and Curriculum Development.

Marzano, R. J., Boogren, T., Heflebower, T., Kanold-McIntyre, J., & Pickering, D. (2012). *Becoming a reflective teacher*. Bloomington, IN: Marzano Research Laboratory.

Marzano, R. J., & Brown, J. L. (2009). *A handbook for the art and science of teaching*. Alexandria, VA: Association for Supervision and Curriculum Development.

Marzano, R. J., & Heflebower, T. (2012). *Teaching and assessing 21st century skills*. Bloomington, IN: Marzano Research Laboratory.

Marzano, R. J., & Toth, M. D. (2013). *Deliberate practice for deliberate growth: Teacher evaluation systems for continuous instructional improvement*. West Palm Beach, FL: Learning Sciences Marzano Center.

Marzano, R. J., & Toth, M. D. (2014). *Teaching for rigor: A call for a critical instructional shift*. West Palm Beach, FL: Learning Sciences Marzano Center.

National Governors Association Center for Best Practices & Council of Chief State School Officers. (2010). *Common Core state standards*. Washington, DC: Author.

Ocasio, T. L., & Marzano, R. J. (2015). *Examining reasoning: Classroom techniques to help students produce and defend claims*. West Palm Beach, FL: Learning Sciences International.

Silver, H. F., Dewing, R. T., & Perini, M. J. (2012). *The core six essential strategies for achieving excellence with the Common Core*. Alexandria, VA: Association for Supervision and Curriculum Development.

William, D. (2011). *Embedded formative assessment*. Bloomington, IN: Solution Tree Press.

Index